FAIR TAXATION IN A CHANGING WORLD

Report of the Ontario Fair Tax Commission

HIGHLIGHTS

Published by University of Toronto Press in cooperation with the Ontario Fair Tax Commission

UNIVERSITY OF TORONTO PRESS

Toronto Buffalo London

Printed in Canada

ISBN 0-8020-7573-8

Printed on recycled paper

Canadian Cataloguing in Publication Data

Ontario. Fair Tax Commission
    Fair taxation in a changing world: report of the Ontario Fair Tax Commission: highlights

Co-published by the Ontario Fair Tax Commission.
Issued also in French under title: Une fiscalité équitable dans un monde en perpétuel changement : points saillants du rapport de la Commission de l'équité fiscale de l'Ontario.
ISBN 0-8020-7573-8

1. Taxation – Ontario. I. Title.

HJ2460.O5O52 1993   336.2'009713   C94-930174-4

This document and the full report are available in French through:

Publications Ontario
    Bookstore:
    880 Bay Street, Toronto

    Mail orders:
    50 Grosvenor Street
    Toronto, Ontario
    M7A 1N8

    Telephone (416) 326-5320
    Toll-free 1-800-668-9938

CONTENTS

ACKNOWLEDGEMENTS 1

THE COMMISSION 2

HIGHLIGHTS OF OUR RECOMMENDATIONS 3

WHAT DO WE MEAN BY FAIRNESS? 7
Fairness and the level of taxation 7
Fairness and the tax policy process 8
Tax fairness among individuals 9
Assessing tax fairness in Ontario 12

CONSTRAINTS ON TAX REFORM IN ONTARIO 15
Mobility of real economic activity 15
Mobility of tax bases 16
Taxation of income from capital: The gap between fair and feasible 17

OUR GENERAL PERSPECTIVE 18

ENHANCING DEMOCRATIC ACCOUNTABILITY 20
The budget process 20
Accounting for tax expenditures 21
Earmarking 22

PAYING OTHER PEOPLE'S TAXES: PROBLEMS OF COMPLIANCE 23
Taxation of business expenses 23
Tax evasion: The underground economy 24

RENEGOTIATING THE TAX COLLECTION AGREEMENTS 26

EQUALITY OF WOMEN AND MEN 28
The tax unit 28
The marital credit 29
Child support payments and alimony 30

SOCIAL POLICY ISSUES AND THE TAX SYSTEM 32
Low-income households in Ontario 32
Taxes and poverty 33
A simplified tax credit system 34
Child care 35
People with disabilities 36
Seniors and taxes 38
Retirement savings 39

MAKING THE TAX SYSTEM MORE PROGRESSIVE 41
The basis for progressive taxation 41
How income and wealth are distributed 41
Options for a more progressive tax system 43

Contents

THE TAX SYSTEM AND ECONOMIC ACTIVITY IN ONTARIO 53
Corporate taxation in a fair tax system 53
Tax expenditures and corporate minimum taxes 55
Payroll taxation 58
The taxation of small business 60
The taxation of cooperatives 62
Resource taxation 63

SALES TAX 67
Sales taxes and ability to pay 67
Taxation of business inputs 68
Reducing compliance and administration costs 69
A national sales tax 69
Luxury taxes 72

FACING THE ENVIRONMENTAL COSTS OF OUR BEHAVIOUR 73
The use of tax instruments for environmental protection 73
A carbon tax 74
Road-use charges and fuel taxes 75
A tax on ozone-depleting substances 76
Environmental user charges 76

PROPERTY TAXES IN LOCAL GOVERNMENT FINANCE 79
Property taxes and tax fairness 80
A new system for funding education 84
Assessment and property tax reform 88
Benefit taxation and local finance 95

PROVINCIAL PROPERTY TAXATION 100
Impact of a provincial commercial and industrial property tax 100
Assessment 101
Rate structure 102
Exemptions 102
Farming property 102

A NEW TAX MIX DESIGN 103

ABORIGINAL PEOPLE AND TAXATION IN ONTARIO 107

IMPACT, IMPLICATIONS AND TRANSITION 109
Impact of our recommendations 109
Implications for intergovernmental relations 111
Implementation and transition 115

APPENDICES
Recommendations 117
References 132

ACKNOWLEDGEMENTS

Our report would never have been possible without the contributions of the many people who wrote to the commission, appeared at our public hearings, served as special advisers, wrote reports, and took the time to participate in consultations. Volunteers across the province organized workshops and community forums; others organized tax forces to meet and discuss tax reform so they could make an effective, informed contribution to our public hearings.

People who participated in the commission's eight working groups and two technical advisory groups deserve special mention. Their persistence and hard work provided us with an invaluable resource. These groups sparked a public debate about tax issues in the communities where we focused our consultation efforts.

We are grateful for the dedication and commitment of these volunteers, as well as the participation by people in the Ontario public service who shared their knowledge and their time with us.

People from the Ministry of Finance, the Ministry of Municipal Affairs, the Ministry of Education and Training, and the Ministry of Agriculture and Food worked closely with us, both at the secretariat and in communities across the province during our public consultation program. Their participation was integral to our work.

We also want to extend our sincere appreciation to the staff, who provided support, information, and resources both to the working groups and to the commission itself. In particular, we thank Hugh Mackenzie, whose vision and leadership as executive director shaped our work and was essential to the smooth functioning of the commission. We are also grateful to Bob Cooke, our director of administration; Barbara Ostroff, who directed the public consultation program; and our director of communications, Dianna Rienstra.

Under the guidance of Allan Maslove, our research director, the consultants who worked with us in our research program leave a valuable legacy of studies, data, and other information designed to contribute to the tax policy process well beyond the conclusion of the commission.

We also wish to express our appreciation to the minister of finance, Floyd Laughren, for his belief that a review of the fairness of Ontario's tax system was long overdue. We would like to commend him particularly for his conviction that tax fairness should be discussed by the people it affects the most.

Some commissioners have registered their dissent from particular recommendations, or made personal comments on them. These are reproduced in the full report.

Finally, on a personal note, I would like to thank all of the commissioners for their hard work and dedication to the project.

Monica Townson
Chair
1 December 1993

THE COMMISSION

HIGHLIGHTS OF OUR RECOMMENDATIONS

Education finance reform for student and taxpayer equity

The commission recommends a new system for financing elementary and secondary education in Ontario, with four key elements:

- Provide full provincial funding of education at a standard capable of meeting Ontario's objectives for elementary and secondary education.

- Replace the $3.5 billion raised from residential property taxes as a source of core funding for education at the provincial standard with funding from provincial general revenues, principally personal income tax.

- Replace the local non-residential property tax for education with a provincial commercial and industrial property tax levied at a uniform rate across Ontario.

- Provide for a local levy on residential property at the discretion of the school board, to be limited to 10 per cent of each board's provincial funding, to pay for local services beyond the provincial standard.

Federal/provincial tax changes for a more progressive and more effective tax system

- Introduce a national wealth transfer tax.

- Eliminate tax expenditures for capital gains and dividend income.

- Negotiate a new federal/provincial income tax agreement to permit Ontario to control the rate schedule, the tax credit system, and the delivery of social and economic policies through the personal income tax system.

- Establish a national sales tax modelled on the GST.

- Provide for greater national harmonization of corporate taxation, with limits on provincial rates and elimination of provincial-level tax preferences.

A new provincial tax credit system to improve tax benefits for the poor

- Replace the current provincial sales, seniors, and property tax credits and the Ontario Tax Reduction program with separate adult and child income-tested refundable benefits.

- Fold the child tax credit into the provincial child benefit program if the structure of the social assistance reforms is changed as proposed by the provincial government.

Increased reliance on environmental taxation

- Increase the use of taxation as a method to address environmental concerns.

- Expand the existing Tax for Fuel Conservation and adjusted rates to encourage the purchase of fuel-efficient vehicles.

- Introduce environmental taxes on carbon dioxide emissions and ozone-depleting substances.

- Reform road-use and fuel taxes.

- Introduce deposit/return taxes on food and beverage containers.

Limited changes in corporate taxation

- Establish a new cash flow tax on mining to replace profits tax as a way to tax the underlying value of Ontario's mineral resources.

- Maintain the present general levels of corporate income taxation.

- Eliminate the preferential corporate income tax rate for manufacturing and processing.

- Eliminate the preferential rate of Employer Health Tax for payrolls under $400,000.

- Introduce new disclosure and accountability requirements for corporate tax expenditures; eliminate Ontario-only corporate income tax expenditures; and address the issue of profitable corporations paying no tax through restrictions on tax expenditures rather than through a corporate minimum tax.

Municipal finance reform

- Abandon market value as the basis for assessment reform; base the assessment of residential property on unit value (physical characteristics weighted to reflect value in current use as reflected in rental value), and base non-residential assessment on rental value.

- Redesign the local finance system to give municipalities a limited right to set tax rates on residential and non-residential property independently.

- Eliminate all private sector exemptions from local property taxation, based on the principle that exemptions from paying for local services should be strictly limited; require full payment in lieu of local taxes by the province for provincial properties and properties exempted by provincial legislation.

- Reduce provincial grants for strictly local services.

- Revise the approach to the sharing of upper-tier (county, regional, district, and metropolitan) municipal costs among lower-tier (local) municipalities.

- Eliminate education development charges for funding infrastructure.

- Increase reliance on user charges for environmental services.

A fairer, more open, tax policy process

- Introduce an open approach to pre-budget consultation, with full disclosure of participants and positions.

- Limit the application of the practice of budget secrecy to permit broader access to policy development within the government and outside; subject most budget decisions to the same degree of secrecy as normal cabinet decisions.

- Review tax expenditures on exactly the same basis as corresponding direct expenditures.

- Restrict earmarking of tax revenues to specific, clearly defined areas.

See Appendix A for a complete list of our recommendations.

Highlights
of Recom-
mendations

WHAT DO WE MEAN BY FAIRNESS?

In the public finance literature, tax fairness has a very specific meaning, referring to the distribution of the burden of taxes among individuals. For the public, tax fairness is a multidimensional concept reflected in different ways in the tax system and in discussions of tax policy. Tax fairness encompasses the overall level of taxes, the perceived value of the services that are funded from tax dollars, the fair distribution of the tax burden based on individuals' ability to pay, the appropriate linkage for the individual between a tax and the service it pays for, and the accessibility of the tax policy process.

Fairness and the level of taxation

Many people feel that the most unfair thing about taxes is that they are too high. In our public hearings, many people expressed the view that "there's no such thing as a fair tax," and subjected the commission to some gentle criticism for its name. This view of the tax system is partly a consequence of the constrained economic circumstances faced by individuals and by governments in the 1990s. The economic crunch in Ontario is real and it is widespread. When pay cheques are shrinking, people are much more conscious of the amount that comes off the top in taxes, and much more concerned about how that money is spent by governments.

This view is also fostered by a tendency in public debate on tax issues to separate taxes from the public services they pay for. Contrived media events such as "tax freedom day" carry the message that taxes impose a burden on individuals that is unrelated to the benefits they receive from public services such as health or education or roads.

"Ninety per cent of the conversation around town, in barbershops and schools, is about expenditures."
~ Hearings participant, Timmins

We found that people are prepared to pay higher taxes if, in return, they receive public services that contribute to a better quality of life. They strenuously oppose higher taxes if they think the money is wasted. In fact, people believe that no tax can be seen as fair if the money raised from it is wasted. This concern led many hearings participants to suggest greater reliance on such measures as specific fees tied to the use of some public services, particularly where environmental issues are considered, and earmarking of revenues raised from some taxes for the provision of identified public services.

Although the level of taxation and the character of the services taxes pay for were not part of the mandate of the Fair Tax Commission, we believe that a better understanding of the relationship between taxes and public services is essential to the development of a constructive debate over issues of tax fairness.

The words of US Supreme Court justice Oliver Wendell Holmes, "Taxes are the price we pay for a civilized society," highlight the importance of maintaining the link between taxes and services in public debate over tax fairness and underline the relationship between the taxes we pay and the kind of society we want. The size of Canada's public sector places Canada in the middle range of countries in the OECD (Organisation for Economic Co-operation and Development) – below countries which provide both a very broad range of public services and comprehensive income security programs, but substantially above a number of countries, including the United States, which provide a narrower range of public services and more limited income security systems.

However, for most Canadians, the United States is the usual point of comparison of taxes and public services. As reflected in the role of the public sector in Canada compared with that in the United States, Canadians and Americans have chosen different kinds of "civilized societies," in that the public sector plays a much more important role in Canada than it does in the United States. In 1989 the public sector accounted for approximately 44.0 per cent of gross domestic product (GDP, or the sum of all goods and services produced in the economy) in Canada compared with 36.4 per cent in the United States. Canadians collectively have decided to provide a higher proportion of the goods and services they require through government than have Americans. This difference is largely because the health care system and the

"People have to stop thinking of taxes as a drain. They are a means by which we demonstrate our responsibility to each other in a society."
~ Hearings participant, Toronto

education system in Canada are, to a significant degree, more public than they are in the United States and because transfers to people through public programs are much more significant relative to GDP in Canada than they are in the United States.

If the role of the public sector in health, education, and transfers to people in Canada were the same as in the United States, the Canadian public sector would be 6.9 percentage points smaller as a proportion of GDP than it is at present. If, in contrast, the public sector played the same role in these areas in the United States as it does in Canada, the US public sector would be 7.4 percentage points larger as a proportion of GDP than it is at present. Taken together, the differences in 1989 between Canada and the United States in transfers to people and in the funding of health and education accounted for more than 90 per cent of the difference in the relative size of the public sector between the two countries.

It is a fantasy to suggest we can have taxes in Canada that compare with those in the United States and, at the same time, provide a significantly higher level of public services. The consequence is our taxes must be higher than those in jurisdictions that do not provide those services.

Fairness and the tax policy process

We found that people are not prepared to accept as fair a tax they do not understand. In our report, we emphasize the need to open up the taxation policy process to make it clearer to and more easily understood by taxpayers. What the tax statutes say is only part of attaining a fair tax system. Fairness in taxation is also about how the statutes are developed and how they are administered. Accessible information and open debate over policy options help people to under-

What do we mean by fairness?

stand and to have confidence that policy choices are fair, even for those who oppose the choices made. Openness promotes "civic discovery" (Reich 1988, 144) or public learning, an important aspect of fairness in itself.

Tax fairness among individuals

There are two broad approaches to fairness in the taxation of individuals: fairness based on some measure of people's ability to pay and fairness based on the benefits people receive from government services. From the perspective of the ability-to-pay approach, a fair tax system will distribute the net burden of taxation in accordance with the ability to pay of individuals or families. The benefit approach views fair taxation as an exchange process whereby taxes are paid in accordance with benefits received from government-provided goods and services.

Ability-to-pay principle

Taxation based on ability to pay implies two propositions about the division of the tax burdens within society: people in similar economic circumstances should pay similar amounts of tax; and people in different economic circumstances should pay different amounts of tax.

The idea that people in similar circumstances should pay similar amounts of tax is firmly rooted in our political culture. People compare themselves to their neighbours. They believe it is unfair that someone whose living standard is similar to theirs should be able to get away with paying less tax because their consumption patterns differ, because their incomes receive different tax treatment, because they have more opportunities to avoid paying tax, or because they are able to escape detection of tax fraud.

This common-sense proposition is known as the principle of horizontal equity – the idea of tax fairness that suggests that taxpayers with the same ability to pay should pay the same tax.

The second proposition, that people in different economic circumstances should pay different amounts of tax, or vertical equity, is much more difficult to define because it requires a judgment as to how different the amounts of tax paid by people in different economic circumstances should be.

In making these value judgments, it is useful to consider the fundamental arguments in favour of taxation that varies according to differences in ability to pay. These arguments flow from scholarly writings on distributive justice, or "the distribution of economic benefits and burdens" in society (Arthur and Shaw 1978, 5).

The literature on distributive justice gives rise to two arguments in favour of taxation that varies according to ability to pay. One is based on the proposition that the goal of a society is to maximize the well-being of the society as a whole. This implies that all taxpayers should make an equal sacrifice of well-being or satisfaction in meeting their tax obligations. The other is based on the proposition that a fair distribution of the economic resources in society would be more equal than the current distribution, and suggests that the tax system has a role to play in alleviating this inequity.

To understand the concept of equal sacrifice requires clarification of the meaning of equal. One can distinguish among equal absolute, equal proportional, and equal marginal sacrifice. The implication of equal proportional sacrifice is that taxes should be proportional to ability to pay. This can be interpreted as an argument for a so-called flat tax – an income tax that applies at the same rate regardless of income.

The general view in the literature on distributive justice, however, is based on the idea that as people's income increases, the value they place on an additional unit of income decreases and that, therefore, the sacrifice associated with paying a given amount of tax declines as income increases. As one economist stated, "a millionaire minds less about the gain or loss of a dollar than I do, and I than a pauper" (Hare 1978, 125). The implication of this logic is that a fair distribution of the tax burden requires that all taxpayers make an equal marginal sacrifice, and that this can only be achieved through taxation that increases in proportion to income as income increases – or progressive taxation.

Arguments based on the desirability of a more equal distribution of economic resources in society point more directly towards progressive taxation, either because they require that tax burdens of those with lower incomes be alleviated or because they require a more equal distribution generally. Taxation that increases less than proportionally as income increases, or regressive taxation, actually makes the distribution of income more unequal. Proportional taxation has no effect on the distribution of income. Only progressive taxation can result in a distribution of income that is more equal after tax than it was before tax.

Both of these lines of argument support progressive taxation. Although these arguments are conceptually different, however, as a practical matter it is impossible to draw a distinction between progressive elements of tax structure required for tax fairness and progressive elements required for the tax system to function as an instrument for income redistribution. Any progressive tax is redistributive.

In tax reform exercises over the last decade or so, principles of vertical equity as reflected in progressive taxation have taken a back seat to concerns about the economic impact of high tax rates on the economic behaviour of high-income individuals. These arguments suggest that it is not economically efficient to impose disincentives on those in our society with the highest incomes. As a result of these recent reforms, the marginal tax rates on higher-income individuals have been reduced in many countries. In addition, to varying degrees, there has been movement away from a progressive rate structure, in which rates on additional income increase as income increases, to a flatter structure, in which the rate on additional income is the same, regardless of the level of income.

We recognize that in a progressive system, marginal tax rates on the highest-income taxpayers must be a matter of concern. Nonetheless, we have concluded that a fair tax system is one based primarily on the ability-to-pay principle, and that, in turn, requires the overall tax system to be progressive. In addition, throughout our public consultation process, we found that most Ontarians believe in progressive taxation. While they disagree about the extent to which the tax system should be made more progressive, they believe that people should contribute proportionally more to support public services as the resources available to them increase.

Benefit principle

A different perspective on the meaning of tax fairness was expressed in the debate about the appropriateness of using local property taxes to pay for education. A common sentiment expressed by the public was that services like elementary and secondary education, which are seen as entitlements in a liberal democratic society, should be funded from taxes related to ability to pay. People argued against the use of property taxes for the funding of education on the grounds that the residential property tax is not related to ability to pay. This debate raised the issue of the fairness of taxes that are linked to benefits received by taxpayers from specific public services.

The benefit principle is thought of as a useful way of allocating the costs of public services, but only those costs that are divisible among individuals. In effect, the tax becomes a kind of user fee. Benefit-based taxes may be linked directly to services, in which case the analogy with market prices is also quite direct. For example, tolls on freeways can be determined on the basis of the distance travelled; user fees can be charged for recreation facilities such as municipal swimming pools and golf courses; and tuition fees can be assessed on students enrolling in public educational institutions. Other benefit-based taxes may be less tightly linked to particular public services. Instead, a tax may be determined to approximate the benefits received from a combination of government-provided goods and services. The property tax may be the best example to the extent that the services funded from the taxes are related to the use or ownership of property, either residential or non-residential, in the municipality.

However, the types of services for which a benefit-based tax would be fair are not typical of most public services. There are at least four categories where one would not want to rely on taxes determined solely on the benefit principle, and where the applicability of this rule is limited.

First, in many situations the benefits conferred by public services cannot be attributed to particular individuals or groups of individuals. These benefits are more general in nature, and there is no reliable method of allocating benefits among individuals. Examples include the benefits of national defence services, large-scale environmental programs,

and some aspects of public health services.

Second, for some government services it may be possible to identify direct beneficiaries, but at the same time significant benefits from these services accrue to society more generally. Thus, while in principle benefit taxes could be levied on primary beneficiaries, in light of these "spillovers" into the larger society it would be neither fair nor efficient to make direct beneficiaries bear the full costs of the services. Examples include education and public transit.

Third, some government programs are undertaken specifically for the purpose of redistribution, and there clearly would be no point in having the beneficiaries pay for their own benefits. This group includes programs such as social assistance, Old Age Security, and other transfer programs.

Finally, society has decided that some public services should be provided to individuals as a matter of right and that no direct fees or benefit taxes should be related to them for that reason. Such taxes would inhibit access to these services and would dilute the universal right to their consumption, especially for lower-income individuals and families. It would be inappropriate to finance essential services in this way, even if it were technically possible to assign benefits to individuals and to link those services to benefit taxes. The most important examples of the application of this principle in Canada are the universal health care system and universal public elementary and secondary education.

We believe that while individual taxes based on the benefit principle of fairness may be appropriate in some circumstances, the tax system as a whole must be fair in the sense that those who have a greater capacity to pay taxes should contribute a greater share of the cost of general government services.

Assessing tax fairness in Ontario

Our fairness objectives can be described in three propositions. Taxes should increase as a proportion of income as income increases – they should be progressive. People in similar economic circumstances should pay similar amounts of tax. And benefit taxation should be limited to those services for which a direct link between a tax or user fee and the use of the service by the taxpayer is appropriate.

We address issues arising from differences in taxes paid by individuals in similar economic circumstances in the context of each individual tax. Issues related to the links between taxes and services also arise in particular taxes such as property taxes and environmental taxes.

The relationship between taxes and income – the progressivity of the tax system – emerges both in our discussions of individual taxes and as we consider the fairness of the tax system as a whole. The tax system consists of a number of different taxes. Some are progressive – they increase in proportion to income as income increases. Some are regressive – they decrease in proportion to income as income increases. The progressivity of the tax system of the whole is influenced not only by the progressivity or regressivity of the individual taxes in the system but also by the relative importance of regressive and progressive taxes in the tax mix.

A measurement of the overall fairness of the system – a fairness audit – must take into account each of these factors. It must measure both the relationship between taxes and the income for individual taxes. And it must also measure the combined effect of all the taxes in the system.

In a formal or legal sense, taxes are levied on both people and institutions in various capacities. Corporations, for example, pay taxes based on their profits, on their payrolls, on some of the goods they purchase, and, in some businesses, on other aspects of their operation as well. However, when considering whether a particular tax, or an array of taxes, is fair, it is necessary to get behind the legal responsibility for payment of taxes and to focus on who actually pays the taxes.

In the final analysis, all taxes are paid by individuals, not institutions. Corporations, for example, exist as legal creations. To determine who actually bears the burden of taxes levied on corporations, one must look to the individuals who are affected by the operation of the corporation. For example, the owners (shareholders) may pay the tax because they receive smaller returns on their investments than they would have without the tax. Alternatively, the purchasers of the corporation's products may pay the tax in the sense that they pay higher prices than otherwise would have been the case. Finally, the tax may result in lower wages and benefits for the people who work for the company than they would have received, and in this sense the employees can be said to pay the tax. When we speak of tax fairness among individuals it is in reference to this ultimate distribution of taxes, after allowing for the impact of taxes on institutions, prices, wages, and return on investments.

We have measured the impact of taxes on Ontarians by expressing the average amount of tax paid as a percentage of income by income decile group. Each decile group represents 10 per cent of Ontario households based on income level. For example, decile 1 includes the 10 per cent of Ontario households with the lowest income and decile 10 includes the 10 per cent with the highest income. (The income ranges associated with the decile groups in figures 1 and 2 are set out in a note to figure 1.)

FIGURE 1

TAXES AS A PERCENTAGE OF AVERAGE INCOME, ONTARIO, 1991

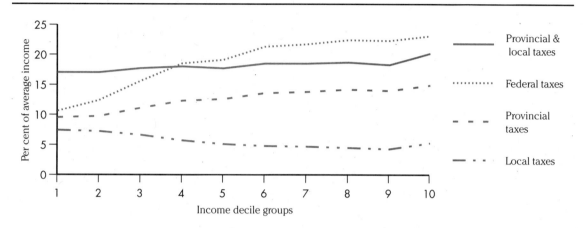

Source: Sheila Block and Richard Shillington, "Incidence of Taxes in Ontario in 1991," in *Taxation and the Distribution of Income,* ed. Allan M. Maslove, Fair Tax Commission, Research Studies (Toronto: University of Toronto Press, forthcoming).

Note: The estimated ranges for the 10 income decile groups in Ontario in 1993 are:

1	Under $12,952	6	$44,599–$53,104
2	$12,952–$20,076	7	$53,105–$62,957
3	$20,077–$28,345	8	$62,958–$76,425
4	$28,346–$35,839	9	$76,426–$99,950
5	$35,840–$44,598	10	$99,951 and over.

Figure 1 compares the average amount of federal, provincial, and local tax paid by Ontario households as a percentage of income in 1991. It shows that taxes levied by the federal government were progressive over the first eight decile groups – the proportion of income paid in federal taxes increases slightly as income increases. The average tax rate rose from about 11 per cent in the first group to 22 per cent for the eighth group. Between the eighth and tenth decile groups the average federal tax rate fluctuated between 22 and 23 per cent. Taxes levied by the Ontario government were also progressive, but only mildly so and only over the first six decile groups. Provincial taxes accounted for about 10 per cent of average income in the first decile group, rising to about 14 per cent in the sixth decile group. However, the aver-

age amount of tax paid fluctuated between 14 and 15 per cent in the seventh to tenth decile groups. In contrast to federal and provincial taxes, local taxes were regressive in all but the last income decile group – the proportion of income paid in local taxes falls as income increases. On average, local taxes represented about 7 per cent of income in the first decile group, falling to about 4 per cent in the ninth group, then rising to about 5 per cent in the tenth group. Because of the interaction of the regressivity of the local tax system and the slight progressivity of the provincial tax system, the combined provincial and local tax systems in 1991 were roughly proportional to income over the first nine decile groups, making up between 17 and 18 per cent of average income in each of these decile groups.

FIGURE 2
SELECTED TAXES AS A PERCENTAGE OF AVERAGE INCOME, ONTARIO, 1991

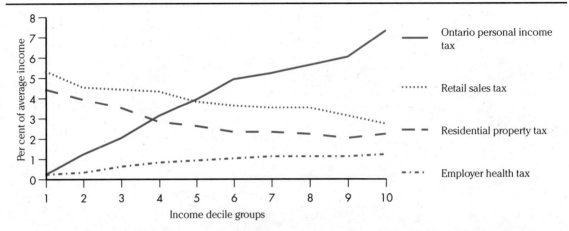

Source: Sheila Block and Richard Shillington, "Incidence of Taxes in Ontario in 1991," in *Taxation and the Distribution of Income,* ed. Allan M. Maslove, Fair Tax Commission, Research Studies (Toronto: University of Toronto Press, forthcoming).

The "tax mix" in Ontario, which includes taxes levied by the provincial government and by local governments, is made up of both progressive and regressive taxes. Figure 2 shows the major taxes levied on individuals in Ontario and the proportion of average income they constituted in each of the 10 income decile groups in 1991. The Ontario personal income tax is the only tax in the mix that is progressive across all income decile groups, making up less than one-fifth of 1 per cent of average income in the lowest income decile and over 7 per cent in the highest. In contrast, the retail sales tax is regressive across all income deciles. In 1991 those in the lowest income decile spent, on average, just over 5 per cent of their income in RST, while those in the highest decile spent just under 3 per cent. Similarly, the proportion of income spent in residential property tax declined as income increased from about 4 per cent in the lowest income decile group to about 2 per cent in the highest. The Employer Health Tax had a slightly

progressive pattern over the first 40 per cent of the income distribution, but was essentially proportional to income over the last six decile groups. These results show that the overall impact of taxes in Ontario can be made more progressive by changing the mix of taxes to rely less on regressive taxes, such as residential property tax, and more on progressive taxes, such as the personal income tax.

It is important to put this general analysis of the incidence of the tax system into perspective. The analysis does not present a detailed picture of how each individual tax affects people, nor does it point to specific prescriptions for change. These results present a general picture of the overall impact of the tax system on people with different incomes in Ontario and provide some general guidance as to how the overall mix of taxes might be made more progressive. As we develop and fine-tune specific recommendations for change throughout our report, we draw on more detailed information from other sources.

CONSTRAINTS ON TAX REFORM IN ONTARIO

Our efforts to create a fair tax system are constrained in a number of ways. Some of these constraints are institutional. For example, Ontario is a sub-national jurisdiction in a federal state. Its powers to tax are limited to some extent by the division of powers in the constitution. Ontario's taxation powers are further limited by federal provincial agreements and financial arrangements which achieve efficiencies in tax administration, but which require the province to cede some of its taxing powers to the federal government.

Other constraints are economic. Even without considering the complex interrelationships between Ontario and other jurisdictions in Canada and in other countries, the operation of our own economy places limits on policies for tax fairness.

Taxes do not just raise revenue. They also affect the behaviour of individuals and corporations. Sometimes the impact of taxes on behaviour is deliberate. For example, when taxation is used as a complement to regulation, it is designed to influence the choices made by people and corporations. Similarly, when the tax system is used to deliver subsidies for certain kinds of private expenditures, it is intended to influence the level of spending in those areas. Taxation also influences the behaviour of people in ways that are not intended. It affects the choices people make between consump-

tion and savings, between work and leisure, between investment in machinery and equipment and investment in people. It also affects choices about where to live, where to work, and where to invest in business activities. These influences are unavoidable. And, as long as the public benefit from the programs funded from taxes exceeds the costs of the taxes plus the costs associated with these changes in behaviour, they are manageable in a modern economy. At the same time, however, these influences cannot be ignored in determining fair tax policies. At a minimum, they suggest that, other things being equal, tax policies should be designed to minimize their unintended influences on individual and corporate behaviour.

In the context of Ontario's role in an increasingly interrelated international economy, the potential impact of taxes and tax rates on both economic activity and the ability of the provincial government to raise revenue based on that economic activity is even more clearly defined.

Mobility of real economic activity

Barriers to the mobility of goods and services, capital, and, to a lesser extent, people are breaking down. The evolution of international trading agreements such as the General Agreement on Tariffs and Trade (GATT), as well as regional trading blocs established through the European Community (EC), the Canada–US Free Trade Agreement (FTA), and the North American Free Trade Agreement (NAFTA), has substantially reduced the limitations imposed by national boundaries on the movement of goods and services.

These agreements have also reinforced the trend towards greater international mobility of capital. Although labour in general is not particularly mobile internationally, individuals with specialized skills have become more mobile with the internationalization of economic activity.

To the extent that the tax system either influences, or is perceived by governments to influence, location decisions, governments will have a tendency to respond to the increased mobility of key elements of the economy. At a minimum, they may attempt to eliminate their tax systems as a negative factor in location decisions, or they may go further to use concessionary tax regimes to make their tax systems a positive factor in location decisions.

The threat of mobility of economic activity has two types of impact on the ability of governments to raise money. If tax rates are reduced because economic activity will otherwise migrate to a jurisdiction with lower rates, the effect on government revenues is direct and obvious. If the location of economic activity actually responds to differences in tax rates and if these differences persist, government revenues will be reduced as economic activity and the tax base associated with it migrate. The revenue loss from migration is potentially greater than the amount of tax that would be paid directly by the mobile person or corporation, since taxes paid by suppliers and employees will also be affected.

Mobility of tax bases

Even if economic activity does not move in response to differences in taxes, the increased sophistication and integration of international financial markets and industrial organization makes it much easier for taxpayers to organize their activities to minimize their overall tax liabilities. The activity may not move, but the tax base associated with it may. For example, corporations may organize their finances in order to report profits in a different jurisdiction from the one in which they are located.

Although mobility of the tax base alone is not as serious a problem either for the economy or for the fiscal system as mobility of the economic activity that underlies the tax base, it is much more difficult to monitor, let alone influence or control.

"Capital is as easy to move as a piece of furniture."
~ London Chamber of Commerce,
London hearing

The impact of these developments on tax revenue will vary from tax base to tax base. Consumption tends to be mobile only in border communities in which it is possible to live in one jurisdiction and purchase consumer goods in another. Employment income – the base for payroll taxes – is also a relatively immobile tax base. At the opposite extreme, the ease with which transnational corporations can manipulate prices charged in transactions internal to the corporation (transfer pricing) and arrange international financing to minimize tax liability makes the corporate tax base extremely mobile. Personal income from capital and wealth are potentially as mobile as corporate income and capital through the use of similar tax-avoiding financial arrangements. These arrangements are attractive only for individuals with large wealth holdings or large pools of income from capital.

For very mobile tax bases, the practical reality is that Ontario's tax rates cannot be significantly different from those of jurisdictions into which the tax base can migrate easily. This constrains the ability of Ontario to raise substantially more revenue from such tax bases as corporate income and the personal wealth of the very wealthy than is raised from these bases in Europe, Japan, and, principally, the United States.

To the extent that the size of the public sector in Ontario exceeds that in other jurisdictions, that difference is sustainable only on the basis of differences in the levels of taxation on relatively immobile tax bases – taxes on personal income, property, sales, payroll, and, to a lesser extent, wealth, as well as benefit taxes or user charges. Although, in general, concerns about tax base mobility are not as pressing for these tax bases as they are for corporate income and capital, special attention must be paid in the design of income and wealth taxes to the potential for inter-jurisdictional movement of capital and income from capital as a tax-avoidance technique. For high-income and very wealthy individuals, the incentives may become sufficient to justify the higher cost of organizing personal finances to minimize tax liability. These incentives for tax minimization would obviously be greatest where Ontario seeks to tax at substantially higher rates than other jurisdictions in Canada.

Taxation of income from capital: The gap between fair and feasible

Competitive pressures and the ease with which capital and income flows can be adjusted internationally to achieve the lowest level of taxation combine to create downward pressure on rates of tax on capital.

At least as it affects the issue of the taxation of capital, the impact of the single market in Europe is not fundamentally different from that of the FTA/NAFTA or, more generally, the combined effect of market- and GATT-driven changes in the world economy.

The problem of taxation of income from capital should not simply be accepted as unsolvable. It is an important problem, not only because of its substantive fiscal impact, but also because of its impact on the perceived fairness of a tax system that cannot extract a fair share of tax from capital income. However, the solution to the problem is neither provincial nor national. Recent reviews of corporate taxation contain two basic messages, both of which are relevant for countries like Canada. First, the systems of corporate income taxation currently used in one form or another in most industrialized countries are not well designed to deal with the particular problems posed by a world of highly mobile goods, investment capital, and, increasingly but to a lesser extent, human capital. Second, a significant degree of harmonization of tax rules and agreement on tax rates among jurisdictions is essential if the pressures generated by mobility are not to result in a significant erosion of the ability of governments to raise revenue from capital and income from capital.

These messages in turn point to the need for an agreement on taxation equivalent to GATT for trade. Such an agreement would counter the tendency for tax bases to migrate and for jurisdictions to compete for business investment by driving down tax rates.

Constraints on Tax Reform

Our General Perspective

Our judgment, based on the fairness issues raised by the public and on our assessment of the impact of the tax system on economic behaviour, is that a renewed emphasis on progressive taxation in Ontario tax policy is both desirable and feasible. We also believe there is considerable scope for making the tax system more even-handed in its treatment of people in similar economic circumstances. In writing our report, we took into account concerns about the impact of the tax system on the economic behaviour of individuals and on the performance of the economy. Those concerns had a significant impact on our recommendations in a number of areas. In keeping with our fairness mandate, however, we saw our task as one of finding an appropriate balance between the goal of tax fairness and these other concerns.

In our search for that balance, we were influenced by those who participated in our public consultations. The involvement of people who do not normally participate in discussions of tax reform gave a different weight to the constraints on fairness in our work than might have been the case in a more traditional exercise. We noted that the concerns that have dominated the public finance literature over the past 20 years, about the impact of taxes on behaviour and therefore on the well-being of individuals, are not always the issues about which

people in Ontario are most worried.

At the same time, we recognize that Ontario faces practical limits on its ability to increase the progressivity of its tax system. The mobility of corporations and, to some extent, of high-income individuals made possible by the integration of the international economy does not support the single-minded pursuit of tax fairness by individual nations, much less by provinces. Levels of taxation in excess of international norms in these areas are difficult to sustain. We believe, however, that Ontario cannot afford to allow passive acceptance of international trends to undermine the capacity of government to provide the public services that Ontarians and Canadians want and to pay for them in a way that is consistent with broadly accepted public standards of fairness. Ontario and Canada should push against those limits, adopting policies that achieve the fairest possible tax system and that strengthen Canada's ability to resist international pressures for minimal taxation of income from capital.

In developing recommendations, we addressed issues in the design of individual taxes as well as the role of each individual tax in the tax system as a whole. For individual taxes, we deal with issues that arise from basic structure as well as from the use of the tax to support other public policy objectives and its impact on tax fairness. Our report raises questions about the extent to which the tax system is used to deliver subsidies to individual and corporate taxpayers. We note that the decision-making process that leads to the implementation of many such tax provisions is flawed, that accountability for the costs of and benefits from these provisions is almost non-existent, and that the widespread use of the tax system to deliver subsidies to individual taxpayers is a major contributor to perceptions that the tax system itself is unfair. While we do not recommend that the tax system not be used to deliver subsidies at all, we recommend that the government introduce much tighter accountability for tax expenditures as a permanent feature of the tax policy process. We recommend that some tax expenditures be taken out of the tax system and delivered through direct spending programs, and that others be redesigned to be more effective in achieving their objectives.

Ontario levies a variety of different taxes, some of which are progressive, others, regressive, and still others that bear no systematic relationship to ability to pay because they are designed to achieve other public policy purposes. We believe that it is appropriate and advisable for Ontario to levy a variety of different taxes and that it is not necessary for every tax to satisfy a specific ability-to-pay criterion. With a variety of different types of taxes, however, the extent to which Ontario relies on each of the major taxes becomes critical in determining the fairness of the system as a whole. In fact, changes in tax mix will have a far greater impact on the fairness of the tax system than would the redesign of any individual tax. In our recommendations, the most important step Ontario can take to improve the relationship between taxes and the ability to pay of taxpayers is to reduce this province's dependence on local property taxes as a source of funding for education and to replace the revenue forgone by increasing revenue from more progressive taxes.

Taxes not intended to be related to ability to pay should be limited to areas in which their use is appropriate on general fairness principles. Thus, we recommend that user charges be limited to such services as sewer and water supply and garbage collection and disposal, and not be imposed in areas such as health care. We also recommend that taxes such as environmental taxes, which are intended to achieve objectives other than the raising of revenue, be designed carefully to focus on those other objectives.

It is important to emphasize that we are proposing a change in direction, not a revolution. The limits that Ontario and Canada face in the taxation of sources of income that are mobile, such as capital, are real and cannot be ignored. As a result, while making recommendations that, taken together, constitute an endorsement of a more progressive tax system, we have been careful to put together a set of recommendations that we believe can reasonably be enacted in Ontario, given all the constraints this province faces.

Our General Perspective

ENHANCING DEMOCRATIC ACCOUNTABILITY

In the course of our work, we heard a great deal about government accountability. Members of the public and working group volunteers identified the opening of the taxation policy process and the provision of better and more accessible information about the tax system as crucial elements in improving its fairness.

We focused on three issues: budget secrecy and the budget process; the treatment of spending programs delivered through the tax system in the form of tax expenditures; and proposals for greater reliance on earmarking of taxes for particular programs as a way to enhance accountability.

The budget process

One of the major underlying issues in taxation policy concerns the extent of public involvement in, and awareness of, the determination of tax policy.

Our research shows that specific budget reforms since 1985 have made the process more open; that the strictures of budget secrecy have been loosened but not broken. We believe the next logical step is to remove the last vestiges of budget secrecy. We recommend that the process of budget policy making be carried out under restrictions no tighter than those applicable to other policy questions requiring cabinet decisions. Ontario should restrict the application of the rule of budget secrecy to the details of tax

"Accountability, like electricity, is difficult to define but possesses qualities that make its presence in a system immediately detectable." ~ Royal Commission on Financial Management and Accountability, 1979

changes that take effect on budget night where an individual or an institution might derive financial gain from the information.

The principle of preventing private gain from prior knowledge should not be elevated above other principles, such as opportunities for elected cabinet ministers to be involved in and informed about a key decision of the government. Currently, a very few members of the government are aware of the contents of the budget before it is announced, essentially the minister of finance and the premier. Particularly when tax policy decisions affect other policy areas, it is counterproductive to ignore expertise available to the government in other ministries.

Consultation

Pre-budget consultation with interest groups can, in one sense, be considered to be going on all year as groups are constantly lobbying various ministers for favourable policies and fiscal measures. But these discussions occur formally only in the three months immediately prior to the budget speech.

Our research shows that recent changes by the minister of finance have made the process of consultation prior to a budget more open and more accessible to a wider variety of interest groups.

Democratic Accountability

The enhanced role of the legislature through the Standing Committee on Finance and Economic Affairs has also been helpful, both in providing more access points for the public and in making alternative analyses of budget issues available to the public.

The 1992 experiment of having various interest groups present briefs in a format that permitted the minister of finance to hear the responses of other interest groups has the potential to provide a more accurate picture of consensus and division about the economy. But support could evaporate unless it is accompanied by information and unless all relevant groups have equal opportunities to participate.

We recommend that this participation be a regular part of the Ontario tax policy process and that the list of participants and any formal representations be made public.

Access to information

Improving the quality of information about public finances in Ontario and broadening public access to that information will assist both the public service and outside researchers in maintaining a continuous watch over the tax system and in assessing reform proposals.

We recommend that a central government agency be created and made responsible for maintaining all databases related to provincial or local public finance. Access to provincial data sources should be readily provided to outside researchers and the public, subject to confidentiality provisions.

Accounting for tax expenditures

The use of the tax system to achieve other policy objectives is an issue that receives little public scrutiny in the current system. The costs of subsidies delivered through the tax system that are designed as substi-

tutes for direct spending programs receive attention only when they are introduced. In today's climate of economic restraint, many of the benefits provided through the tax system are therefore protected from the tougher scrutiny and exposure to cuts given to visible direct expenditures.

These subsidies are defined as tax expenditures because they function as tax system equivalents to direct spending programs. These provisions are pervasive in the tax system. For example, the child care expense deduction is a tax expenditure. Rather than providing a tax deduction to parents, which costs the government forgone revenue, cheques could, in principle, be issued to all parents incurring child care expenses. The direct spending equivalent might be to spend comparable amounts providing child care spaces and subsidizing their use.

Another example is the Research and Development Super Allowance in the corporate income tax, which provides an additional deduction of 25 per cent for eligible research and development expenditures incurred in Ontario. The direct spending equivalent would be to make grants to firms undertaking eligible R&D activity.

The issues at stake in choosing between tax expenditures and direct spending should be clarified through the adoption of more transparent accountability provisions and processes. Currently, Ontario does not publish information on tax expenditures on a regular basis, although such information has been assembled to assist the work of the Fair Tax Commission. Tax expenditures are not automatically reviewed either internally through the program review and estimates process or externally through the work of the provincial auditor.

Improvements in the manner in which tax expenditures are developed, adminis-

Democratic Accountability

tered, and evaluated depend on two reforms. First, the tax policy process in general must be made more open and accessible to a broader range of inputs from inside and outside government. Second, tax expenditures should be developed and evaluated using criteria that recognize they are spending programs that happen to be delivered through the tax system. Where special procedures have to be developed, they should be designed to mirror those for direct expenditures.

Tax expenditures should be included in annual program reviews and should be subject to review by the provincial auditor.

Earmarking

Earmarked funds could represent major elements of total public spending that are largely beyond the control of the elected representatives who are accountable to the public.

In recent years, earmarking of funds raised from particular taxes for specific government purposes has been advocated as a solution to a number of different issues in spending and taxation. Earmarking has also been advocated as a way to reduce public resistance to new taxes.

Recently, for example, environmentalists have advocated the earmarking of "green taxes" for environmental purposes. They argue that revenues from environmental taxes should be directed towards environmental programs, partially as a way to secure funding and partially to respond to criticism of environmental levies as "tax grabs" that serve no real environmental purpose. Other arguments are made in favour of earmarking excise taxes related to social concerns.

These arguments do not necessarily suggest a form of pure earmarking. Rather, they may suggest a form of notional earmarking as a signal to the public of the government's concern with the issue.

Governments have, however, run into difficulty with notional earmarking. The issue of the Ontario tire tax, which levied a five-dollar tax on each new tire sold, was raised time and again in our public hearings as an example of the provincial government's failure to direct the revenue generated from the tax to the appropriate activity. The tax, introduced in the 1989 Ontario budget, was justified on the basis that it was required to pay for particular spending programs. It was abolished in the 1993 budget, following a recommendation from the commission's Environment and Taxation Working Group.

We believe the case for earmarking is strongest when the payment of the earmarked tax is closely linked to the consumption of a particular public service. There appear to be few if any advantages, either substantively or in terms of accountability, to loose or notional earmarking.

Ontario should not in general earmark funds raised from particular taxes for the funding of specific government programs. Nor should Ontario create the impression that taxes are earmarked by creating names that describe an expenditure program rather than the base of the tax (for example, by naming its payroll tax the Employer Health Tax). Accountability is not served when revenues are linked only rhetorically to expenditures in order to garner support for the adoption of a new tax.

Earmarking should be limited to those situations in which benefit taxation would be appropriate – namely, where the benefits from a service can be attributed to individuals. It should apply only where redistribution is not an objective in providing the service, where public policy does not require that the service be provided to individual beneficiaries as a right, and where there is a clear relationship between the earmarked fee or tax and the service to be funded.

PAYING OTHER PEOPLE'S TAXES: PROBLEMS OF COMPLIANCE

Compliance is an important element in determining how fair the tax system is for three reasons.

First, a tax that is paid by some of those obliged to pay and not paid by others who are equally obliged to pay is almost by definition an unfair tax. This is particularly true if a taxpayer's ability to avoid or evade taxation is linked to a characteristic such as income, occupation, source of income, or social status. For example, a tax that is easily avoided by higher-income taxpayers or by taxpayers whose income is derived from capital will be less progressive in practice than it appears to be on paper.

Second, the ability of some taxpayers to avoid or evade taxation while others in similar circumstances pay more undermines both basic fairness and the general willingness of taxpayers to comply voluntarily with tax laws. For example, abuse of provisions available to the self-employed may create inequities between employees and self-employed people in otherwise similar economic circumstances and undermine overall confidence in the fairness of the tax system.

Third, every taxpayer's success in avoiding or evading taxation is eventually some other taxpayer's tax increase. This connection has a direct impact on the value-for-money relationship that is central to society's general willingness to pay tax to support common services.

One way to make compliance easier for taxpayers is to keep the system as simple and clear as possible.

Taxation of business expenses

One avoidance issue of particular concern to some at our public hearings was the taxation of business expenses which serve as tax-free "perks" for employees. Examples frequently cited include business meals, attendance at entertainment or sporting events, business or convention travel, home office expenses, and the personal use of a company car or other property of the business. The concern arises because these expenditures are deductible as expenses to the business, but are not recognized as taxable benefits to the individual employees or business operators who benefit from them. This means that employees or business owners who benefit from such perks are in a better position than other employees who receive a taxable salary and

"It is grossly unfair that the wealthy entertain lavishly at the finest restaurants and enjoy the right to deduct expenses from income, while the average citizen who buys a hot dog for lunch from a street vendor with their after-tax income must also pay unfair consumption taxes."
~ Hearings participant, Toronto

purchase the same goods or services out of their after-tax income.

In principle, the way to achieve equity between those who receive these types of benefits and those who do not would be to determine the value of the good or service received and add it to the income of the employee or the business owner for tax purposes. However, this approach would be difficult to apply in practice. For example, in some cases it would be very difficult to distinguish between perks enjoyed by employees of a firm and those enjoyed by its customers. If customers weren't required to declare their perks on the same basis as employees, the opportunities for abuse would be significant.

The approach that has gradually evolved federally and provincially is to use rules of "rough justice" to allocate these costs between perks that should be taxable to the individual and business expenses that should not, rather than attempting to determine the appropriate allocation on a case-by-case basis. One type of rule provides a formula for determining the benefit taxable to the employee. An example is the so-called stand-by charge for employees who have a company car available for personal use. A taxable benefit of 2 per cent of the capital cost of the car is assessed for each month the car is available for the use of the employee.

Another type of rule limits the deduction by the employer of such expenses. An example is the tax treatment of meals and entertainment expenses, where the employer is allowed to deduct only 80 per cent of the cost of meals and entertainment expenses for federal income tax purposes. In Ontario, beginning in June 1993, only 50 per cent of costs of meals and entertainment expenses are deductible for purposes of the corporate income tax,

although the limit applicable to unincorporated businesses remains at 80 per cent because such businesses are taxed through the personal income tax and are subject to federal tax policy.

We have concluded that the rough justice approach is the most appropriate one to follow in dealing with the difficult issue of employee and owner benefits from business expenditures. The difficulties are compounded because the issues pertain to both the personal and the corporate income taxes, and involve both federal and provincial statutes. Governments should seek to develop a workable and fair set of rules for these expenses. This approach should not be punitive, but should provide a reasonable balance between discouraging use of non-taxable benefits, while allowing continued deduction of the portion that represents actual business costs.

Tax evasion: The underground economy

When tax avoidance becomes tax evasion, the taxpayer crosses the line between legitimate economic activity and the "underground economy." The underground economy is a phrase used to describe economic activity in which taxpayers fail to report income or sales for tax purposes, either completely or in part, and thereby practise tax evasion.

> *"Escalation of the underground economy is happening because the tax system is perceived as unfair."*
> ~ Submission, Greater Peterborough Chamber of Commerce

Taxpayers are and should be concerned about the extent of such activities. They lead indirectly to higher taxes on legitimate business activities and undermine the fairness of the tax system as it affects individuals.

Problems of Compliance

One approach to the problem of the underground economy is to focus on the kinds of income or activity in which tax evasion is prevalent. A study for the commission points out that tax evasion is more common when no tax is withheld and when reporting of information is not required, suggesting that changes in administration might be the solution. In Australia, for example, tax evasion in the home renovation business has been addressed by requiring homeowners to withhold the tax payable. A similar example might be to require applicants for building permits to indicate on the permit the name of the contractor performing the work. Although this kind of approach may not be appropriate in Ontario, it illustrates the point that enforcement measures may have to be tailored to meet possible underground economy activities.

Another approach is to return to the basic factor that influences tax avoidance behaviour – the taxpayer's perception of the risks and rewards associated with tax avoidance. If aggressive tax avoidance or tax evasion represents a gamble by the taxpayer, the enforcement response should be to increase the probability of inappropriate or illegal behaviour being discovered and/or to increase the potential loss associated with being caught. For the taxpayer, this would both make the odds less favourable and increase the amount at risk.

Research indicates that improving the level of compliance requires more enforcement activities and higher penalties for infractions. However, these prescriptions are costly to the government and have the potential to be offensive to the public. Additional personnel are required to increase the probability of detecting evasion, and larger fines will induce tax evaders to mount more costly defences,

which may also incur more costly prosecutions. For the public, more enforcement means more information requirements, more audits, and, almost certainly, more situations where complying taxpayers are subjected to costs and stress in dealing with the tax administration authorities.

However, the costs to both the government and individual taxpayers must be weighed against costs to society as a whole when unchecked tax evasion causes revenues and confidence in the fairness of the tax system to erode. There is no single policy prescription that will make this phenomenon go away.

We urge the government to increase rates of audit and penalties for non-compliance and to develop additional reporting and withholding requirements. We suggest that the government make the public aware of instances in which evasion has been successfully controlled in order to increase the perceived risk of evasion. Finally, we urge the provincial government to work with the federal government to identify potential underground economic activities and to share information that could be useful in detecting evasion.

> "The tax system is too complex, which creates unnecessarily high compliance costs, continuing uncertainty about tax liabilities and obligations, confusion about tax incidence and inequity. Because the system is largely self-assessed, public acceptance and understanding is essential if the system is to maintain its integrity."
> ~ Submission,
> Ontario Chamber of Commerce, Toronto

Problems of Compliance

RENEGOTIATING THE TAX COLLECTION AGREEMENTS

Ontario, like every province in Canada except Quebec, is part of the Tax Collection Agreements (TCA) for levying the personal income tax. Under the TCA, the federal government collects personal income tax and then remits the provincial portion back to Ontario in a series of payments. There are a number of benefits for Ontario of this arrangement, but also a number of costs, primarily in terms of tax policy flexibility.

The benefits of the TCA to Ontario include: charge-free processing, audit, collection, and prosecution; provincial tax amounts being based on tax assessed, whether collected or not; and cost-reduced processing of provincial tax credit schemes. In addition, the tax harmony achieved by the TCA promotes the free flow of resources and the efficient allocation of capital and labour, thereby increasing Canada's competitiveness in world markets and stimulating economic growth.

At the same time, the restrictions these arguments place on Ontario's tax policy flexibility are very tight. The federal government defines the types of income subject to tax; the deductions from income; exemptions; non-refundable tax credits; tax rates; tax brackets; and indexation factors. The provincial personal income tax (PIT) rate is calculated as a percentage of the Basic Federal Tax.

Ontario must follow the federal model in its legislation, regulations, and interpretations. Ontario accepts as final all decisions of the federal minister of finance without the benefit of consultation or discussion. The federal government has complete power over interpretations and advance rulings.

No interest is credited to Ontario on Ontario PIT collected but not yet paid to the province, nor is interest charged on overpayments of Ontario PIT. The federal government assumes all bad debts for PIT assessed but not collected.

In order to increase the progressivity of the personal income tax at higher income levels, some provinces levy a PIT surtax. As of 1 July 1993, Ontario's surtax is 20 per cent of provincial tax between $5500 and $8000, and 30 per cent of provincial tax in excess of $8000. In addition, provinces can initiate tax reduction programs for individuals with low incomes as Ontario did with the Ontario Tax Reduction program.

Ontario must receive federal approval for any tax credit scheme that induces investment or investor location exclusively in the province. Ontario has received approval for property and sales tax credits, the Ontario Home Ownership Savings Plan credit (which is income tested), and the Ontario investment and employee ownership tax credit. Other provinces offer credits for investment in provincially based companies.

Ontario's lack of policy control over its personal income tax is out of step with the reality that it is the province's largest source of tax revenue.

We recommend that Ontario seek a federal-provincial tax collection agreement that permits Ontario to:

- Levy its tax directly on the income base rather than the "tax on tax" arrangement currently in place, where the provincial tax is levied as a percentage of the federal tax payable.
- Determine the number of rate brackets and the applicable rates independently of the federal government.
- Define, and determine the values of its own tax credits independently of the federal government

These proposals are consistent with the framework put forward for public comment in a 1991 federal government discussion paper.

In addition, we recommend that new tax collection agreements permit the federal and provincial governments to determine their own tax expenditures, independently

of each other. This could be achieved in two ways. Tax expenditures could be converted to credits rather than deductions, exemptions, or exclusions from the base, in which case each level of government could decide the rate of credit to be applied against its own tax. Alternatively, provincial governments could be empowered to add back into their taxable income base any tax expenditure items from the federal system that they did not wish to parallel.

Ontario should seek a federal-provincial tax collection agreement that also gives provincial governments a role in income tax policy and administration commensurate with their growing share of total income tax revenues. Such an agreement would provide for direct input by provincial governments into the audit and enforcement activities of the federal government involving their taxpayers. It would also establish institutional arrangements for formal federal-provincial consultation in advance of any federal decision affecting the definition of the income tax base.

Tax Collection Agreements

EQUALITY OF WOMEN AND MEN

The impact of the tax system on women is different from its impact on men. This differential impact is not the result of any explicit discrimination against women in the Income Tax Act. Nothing in the letter of the law singles out either men or women for special treatment. The income tax has different impacts on women than on men because of the way its provisions interact with differences in the economic position of women and men in society.

Women are less well off than men whether the measure of well-being is total income or earnings from employment, and regardless of the type of household in which they live. In Canada in 1991, women who worked full time for a full year earned an average of 69.6 per cent of the average earnings of men. (The Ontario figure was 69.8 per cent.) The average earnings of women in Canada, both full and part time, are 61.5 per cent of the average earnings of men. Women are more likely to be poor than men and less likely to have high incomes.

These facts have two types of implications for the fairness of the income tax system as it relates to women. First, because women on average earn less than men, women are less able to take advantage of subsidies delivered through the tax system. And even when they are able to take advantage of these provisions, women derive less benefit from them.

Second, because women on average earn less than men, elements of the income tax that affect the economic relationships between people, and that are technically gender neutral, are not neutral in their outcomes. These issues arise most notably in three features of the income tax: the tax unit, the marital amount and non-refundable credit, and the treatment of child support payments and alimony.

We believe that taxation should respect, support, and encourage a woman's economic autonomy. Accordingly, we recommend that the individual be retained as the unit of taxation, that the marital credit be abolished, and that treatment of child support and alimony payments be changed to eliminate the deduction for such payments and to exclude them from the taxable income of the recipient.

The tax unit

The choice of the unit of taxation is a fundamental issue in the design of the income tax system. With the individual as the unit of taxation, individuals are taxed solely on the basis of their own income. If the family is the tax unit, the aggregate income of a group defined by marital/partnership status or by membership in a family group is taxed.

From the perspective of the autonomy of women, the most important argument against changing the tax unit in Canada to the family relates to the impact of such a change on the labour force participation of women. If the family were the unit of taxation, income could be split between the partners in a couple. Combining the income of people with different incomes would increase the marginal tax rate of the lower-income partner. Since the lower-income partner is generally the woman, her earnings would face a higher marginal tax rate than if she were taxed as an individual. This in turn creates a disincentive for women's participation in the labour force and undermines women's goals of economic independence.

We recommend that the individual be retained as the unit of taxation. In addition to recognizing and supporting the autonomy of women, this policy requires neither assumptions about how income is shared within families (taxation of family income implicitly assumes equal sharing) nor decisions about how to define a family. These decisions are becoming more and more difficult as Canadians participate in a variety of family types.

The marital credit

The contrast between the roles actually played by women in the economy and the roles around which the tax system is designed calls into question the basis for tax provisions such as the marital credit and the transferability of other credits between spouses.

In present income tax law, special provisions have been made to reflect the impact of family support obligations on the individual's ability to pay: the married status credit, the equivalent-to-married credit, the dependant credit, and the child care expense deduction.

The marital credit is available to a taxpayer supporting a spouse earning a low income or earning no income. The amount of the credit is reduced by income earned by the spouse with the lower income. In 1993 the maximum value of the federal credit is $914.60, and that amount is reduced as the annual income of the spouse rises above $538. The maximum value of the Ontario portion is $530.47, which gives a maximum total value for an Ontario taxpayer of $1445.07. The credit is primarily claimed by male tax filers with incomes under $50,000. In 1993 it became available to common-law couples as well as married couples.

Compared with all tax filers (based on 1989 data), claimants are under-represented at incomes of less than $30,000 and over-represented in other income ranges, particularly those between $30,000 and $60,000. Half the claimants of the marital credit have dependent children.

Although some see the credit as compensation for household labour, it is not structured as a credit for women's unpaid labour in the home, but as a tax break for dependency. The size of the credit and the fact that it is payable to the husband mean that it does not reward women for household duties. The credit is available regardless of what labour is performed in the home or who does it. It does not recognize the fact that many women assume a double burden when they work outside the home by continuing to provide the bulk of domestic labour in their households in addition to their participation in the workplace.

Assumptions regarding the relationships of adults to each other and the obligations of support between them are clearly changing. Our operating assumption is that the ability of adults to support themselves is unrelated to their relationships. The

Equality of Women & Men

appropriate solution, then, is to abolish the marital credit. To continue the credit institutionalizes the presumptions of dependency of women on men and discriminates between women who work in the home and women who work in the paid labour market as well as in the home.

We can see no reason why the tax system should recognize spousal dependency, especially when it no longer recognizes dependent children and when approximately half the couples claiming the benefit have no dependent children. If the Tax Collection Agreements are amended to permit provincial governments to determine their own credits, we recommend that Ontario abolish the marital credit in its personal income tax and redirect the tax benefits through a reformed credit system.

Child support payments and alimony

In the personal income tax, child support payments by a divorced parent for the support of the children of the dissolved marriage are tax deductible. The parent receiving these support payments is required to declare them as income. Payments of alimony from one divorced spouse to the other are treated the same way.

Because children tend overwhelmingly to become the responsibility of the woman following the dissolution of a marriage, the result is that, for the most part, child support payments are deductible for the father and taxable to the mother.

People who appeared at our hearings argued strongly that it is unfair to treat child support payments as taxable income for the recipient (usually the mother). While we do not question the technical tax argument that if the payment is deductible for the payer it should be taxable in the hands of the recipient, the argument begs

the question of why the payment is deductible in the first place.

In support of the deduction, it is argued that it provides an incentive to divorced parents to fulfil their child support obligations and that, because women tend to earn less than men and therefore face lower marginal tax rates than men, the combined effect of the deduction for support paid and the taxation of support received is to increase the amount of money available for the support of children.

There are, however, two responses to such an argument. First, there is no evidence to suggest that the deduction is an adequate incentive to pay. Seventy-five per cent of support payers in Ontario are to some degree in default, even with the benefit of the deduction.

Second, the effect of federal tax reform in 1988 has been to flatten the rate structure. It is now much less likely that there will be a substantial difference in the marginal rates of tax paid by divorced parents. It is also doubtful that the current policy provides better benefits for children of divorced parents than they would otherwise have.

The deductibility of support payments has to be considered in the context of what governments should be expected to do about ensuring that non-custodial parents meet their obligations, legal or otherwise, to support their children. If governments have a role, then there are far better ways of ensuring that obligations are met than by providing a tax deduction to non-custodial parents.

> *"There is something seriously wrong with a system that financially benefits the non-custodial parent while penalizing the parent with the full responsibility of raising the children. Government has paid lip service to the issue of equity for women in this province. True equity implies economic independence."*
> *~ London*

We do not see why non-custodial parents should receive a subsidy for payments made to support their children when no such subsidy exists in the tax system for parents in intact families. The payment is clearly a personal expense of the payer and, therefore, should not be deductible. The payment is not income to the recipient; it is a reimbursement of costs borne by the custodial parent which both parents are obliged to share.

For women who are receiving both spousal and child support, it may be inequitable and difficult to separate the two types of payments for taxation purposes.

We recommend that Ontario seek the agreement of the federal government to abolish the deduction for child support and alimony payments. The payments should not be taxable in the hands of the recipient. However, we do not recommend Ontario act alone. Federal action is necessary because of cases where one parent lives in Ontario and one outside. If Ontario acted alone to abolish the deduction, then either no taxation or double taxation would result.

Equality of Women & Men

SOCIAL POLICY ISSUES AND THE TAX SYSTEM

The tax system is used extensively to deliver a wide range of social policies. It is seen as a convenient way to deliver program benefits because the administration costs are relatively low. It broadens the reach of programs because most adults file tax returns. In addition, it is well-suited to the delivery of income-tested grants and subsidies, and benefits are delivered anonymously without the stigma often associated with separately delivered social assistance benefits and direct grant programs.

Through federal and provincial social policy commitments, various forms of tax relief and transfer payments are provided to increase the disposable income of specific groups. In addition, the tax system is used as a delivery mechanism for a number of social policy subsidies.

Although these subsidies, or tax expenditures, were all initiated by the federal government and form part of the federal personal income tax structure, the operation of the Tax Collection Agreements automatically makes them Ontario's subsidy programs as well. We address specifically the largest of these programs: the tax deduction for child care expenses; support for people with disabilities and for seniors; and the tax deduction for contributions to RRSPs and pension plans.

We also deal separately with the changes to the Tax Collection Agreements that would

> "Our tax system should be generating enough revenue to stop the painful social and economic crisis that is sweeping across the province ... eliminating poverty should be the primary focus of the tax system."
> ~ Hearings participant, Toronto

be required to give Ontario the policy flexibility to deal with the tax fairness issues arising from these tax-delivered social policies.

Low-income households in Ontario

The problem of low or inadequate incomes is a major social policy issue. Persistently high unemployment, economic restructuring, and the growth in the numbers of low-wage jobs have increased the risk that individuals and families in Ontario will have low incomes.

More than one million people in Ontario lived in low-income households in 1991. This accounted for about 10 per cent of the population of the province. We define low-income households as those with total incomes below the after-tax low-income cut-off (LICO), calculated by Statistics Canada based on family/household size and the population of the area of residence.

Fifty-seven per cent of women and children living in female-led single parent families were poor and were almost six times as likely to live in a low-income household as

FIGURE 3
DISTRIBUTION OF LOW-INCOME
INDIVIDUALS BY HOUSEHOLD TYPE,
ONTARIO, 1991

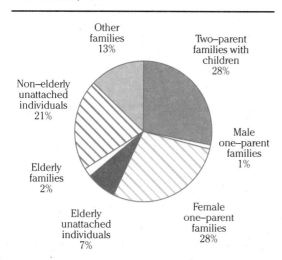

Source: Statistics Canada, Household Surveys Division, Survey of Consumer Finances, unpublished data.

the rest of the population. Almost a quarter of unattached individuals had a low income, and couples with and without children were the least likely to live in poverty.

Almost 60 per cent of low-income individuals lived in families with children, almost half of them in female-led lone parent families. Of the almost 30 per cent of low-income Ontarians who lived alone in 1991, about a quarter were elderly.

Taxes and poverty

Individuals and families with low incomes pay income taxes. In 1991 there were 524,925 people in Ontario who lived in families with income below Statistics Canada's low-income cut-off and who paid income tax. Most people in low-income families pay very small amounts of income tax. For example, the average tax

> *"We have to look beyond the Statistics Canada definition and examine the dynamics of poverty." ~ Hearings participant, London*

paid by families in the $10,000 to $20,000 income range in 1993 in Ontario was $206, 1.4 per cent of their income.

One way to reduce the tax burdens on low-income families is to increase the tax threshold in the personal income tax system. The tax threshold is the level of income at which people start paying tax. In the current income tax structure, the tax threshold is established by tax credits such as those determined by the basic personal amount and the married amount. The distinguishing features of these credits are that they are non-refundable – payable only to the extent that a taxpayer would otherwise owe tax – and that they have the same value to all taxpayers, regardless of their income and regardless of the combined incomes of the members of the household. Because the credits that create the tax threshold apply equally to every taxpayer, increasing these credits is a very costly way to reduce tax burdens on people with low incomes.

The Ontario tax system contains two additional features that serve to reduce tax burdens on people with low incomes. The Ontario Tax Reduction program (OTR) is a non-refundable tax credit that provides tax relief to individuals. The OTR varies with the number of children and the income of the individual taxpayer. The other Ontario tax credits – the property and sales tax credits – are refundable credits, payable whether or not there is taxable income. These credits provide tax relief to families. The credits are based on the number of children in the family, on age and on property taxes or rent, and are income-tested based on family income.

Tax relief for individuals and families

The OTR illustrates clearly the problem of attempting to reduce tax burdens on people with low incomes by using credits based on individual income. Because the OTR is provided to individual taxpayers rather than families, lower-income family members can benefit from the reduction even if they live in families with combined incomes substantially above any low-income threshold.

In addition, the OTR is based on Ontario tax, not income. This means that higher-income earners who pay little Ontario tax because they take advantage of tax expenditures can also benefit from the program.

Our analysis of the distribution of benefits of the OTR in 1993 estimates that just over 10 per cent of the money spent on the program, or $16.2 million, actually goes to families with incomes below $20,000. Just over 16 per cent of the benefit, or $24.6 million, goes to families with incomes in excess of $50,000. The program is obviously not well targeted.

Ontario was a pioneer in Canada in the use of refundable tax credits. Because they are linked to family income rather than individual income, such credits are well targeted to low-income families. In addition, because they are refundable, these credits also increase the income of people who are not liable for income tax. The principal problem with Ontario's refundable credit system is that it is unnecessarily complex. The Ontario sales tax credit, the property tax credit for seniors, and the property tax credit are confusing. Despite their names, they bear little relationship to the amounts of sales tax or property taxes paid.

A simplified tax credit system

The current sales, property, and seniors credit system should be rationalized into an adult credit called the Ontario tax assistance credit (which would provide for a supplementary benefit for individuals over the age of 65) and a child credit. Both

TABLE 1
ONTARIO TAX REDUCTION
(ESTIMATES FOR 1993)

Family income ($)	Gross tax expenditure ($ millions)	% distribution of benefits
10,000 and under	3.3	2.18
10,001–20,000	12.9	8.53
20,001–30,000	51.1	33.80
30,001–40,000	43.1	28.51
40,001–50,000	16.2	10.71
50,001–60,000	9.2	6.08
60,001–70,000	5.2	3.44
70,001–90,000	4.5	2.98
Over 90,000	5.7	3.77
All tax filers	151.2	100.00

Source: Fair Tax Commission estimates based on Statistics Canada Social Policy Simulation Database and Model (SPSD/M).

credits should be refundable and income-tested, based on family income.

The adult credit would provide a benefit of a flat amount per adult. The child tax credit would provide benefits based on number of children. In addition, if Ontario gains control over the non-refundable credits in its income tax in a new tax collection agreement, we propose that the equivalent-to-married credit in the income tax, which provides a tax reduction to single parent families, be replaced with a supplement to the child tax credit for single parent families. This would provide better targeted relief to low-income single parent families. It would also provide benefits to all such families, whether or not they pay tax.

Ontario's tax credits should be simplified and consolidated. The OTR program should be eliminated.

Child benefits

The system of benefits for families with children is currently in a state of flux. The feder-

Social Policy Issues

al government has just completed a series of reforms that eliminated the family allowance program, the refundable child tax credit, and the non-refundable income tax credit for dependent children.

Ontario has also recently announced a major change in direction for reform of its social assistance system. It has proposed that the $1.1 billion in support for children currently delivered through social assistance be rolled into a new income-tested program similar in many ways to the federal Child Tax Benefit. Working poor and other low-income families who do not qualify for social assistance will be eligible for benefits under this program.

> *"All parents should receive recognition financially for the work and money they invest in raising children. The time alone that parents invest could equal a second job."*
> *~ Hearings participant, Toronto*

Our recommendations for tax-delivered assistance to children were developed in the context of the programs existing outside the tax system for the delivery of child benefits. The current social assistance system does not deliver benefits to children of working poor families, and as long as it is the only delivery mechanism in Ontario for child benefits outside the tax system, tax-delivered assistance should be retained.

If reform proceeds in the general direction outlined in the government's proposal for an Ontario Child Income program, however, we see no reason to retain two delivery systems with the same target population. Our recommended child tax benefit should be integrated with it rather than continue as a separate program.

Recent changes that have taken place in the federal system of support for families with children have generated a great deal of controversy. As a result of the elimination of the family allowance program and the non-refundable credit for dependent children, there is currently no program that provides general support for families with children, regardless of income.

We are concerned that these changes signify a retreat from the long-standing view in Canada that children are at least in part a social responsibility. We would have liked to have recommended that Ontario fill the gap left by these federal changes by creating a two-tier child benefit program, one tier of which would be paid regardless of income. We did not do so, however, because we are conscious of the substantial costs that such an approach would entail.

Child care

The child care deduction in the personal income tax allows child care expenses, up to maximum amounts that vary according to the age of the child, to be deducted from taxable income. The 1992 federal budget raised the allowable deduction for child care expenses effective in 1993 from $4000 to $5000 for each child under seven years of age, and from $2000 to $3000 for each child between seven and 14. For a dependent child with a severe mental or physical disability, a family may claim up to $5000 regardless of age. Low-income families who are unable to deduct child care expenses are permitted to claim an additional amount per child under seven years of age ($213 in 1992) through the federal Child Tax Benefit.

The Income Tax Act requires that, where there is more than one supporting adult, the person with the lower income must claim the expense. In order to claim the deduction, the taxpayer must supply receipts, if the care-giver is an institution, or a social insurance number, if the care-giver is an individual.

Social Policy Issues

Although the deduction is often characterized as one related to employment, its primary function is to deliver subsidies for child care. The child care deduction was seen as a critical part of the federal government's national child care strategy in 1988–89, when the announced reason for increasing the deduction was to increase its support for child care.

"The child care expense deduction benefits taxpayers in higher income brackets most, and it only recognizes receipted care. It is important to look at day care from the point of view of the parents who have the primary responsibility."
~ Hearings participant, Kitchener

As a deduction, it provides a larger subsidy to higher-income families with higher marginal tax rates, and no benefit to families with no tax payable. A two-earner family with two children and two high-income earners taxed at a marginal rate of 53 per cent will receive a tax benefit equivalent to $5300 for child care. A two-earner family with two children, where one spouse earns the lower income of $25,000 annually and is taxed at a marginal tax rate of 27 per cent, will receive a tax benefit equivalent to $2700 for child care. The average value of the deduction for families claiming the child care expense deduction in Ontario in 1990 ranged from $140 in the under $10,000 income range to $2120 for those with incomes in excess of $150,000. Low-income families derive little benefit from this program.

The total federal and provincial tax subsidy in Ontario given through the child care deduction was $187 million in 1990. Ontario's portion of this tax subsidy was approximately $63 million. In our view, this money would be better spent outside the tax system on child care services available to all families, regardless of socio-economic status. A direct spending program for child care would also be a more equitable way to support the needs of parents,

whether women or men, for accessible non-parental child care services.

If the Tax Collection Agreements are amended to permit provincial governments to determine their own income tax expenditures, we recommend that Ontario eliminate the child care expense deduction and use the revenue in a direct spending program for child care.

People with disabilities

People with disabilities are among the most disadvantaged in Canada. This disadvantage stems from barriers they face to full participation in social life, especially in employment. Overcoming these barriers entails costs to society and to individuals for wheelchairs and other assistive devices; special medical services, equipment, and medication; transportation; special housing; workplace adaptation; vocational rehabilitation; and attendant care.

We addressed the question of whether tax-based disability support was the best form of support for disability-related costs, or whether there were other mechanisms that would be fairer and more effective.

We are not convinced that the tax system is the appropriate foundation on which to build more generous disability-related assistance for Canadians. As in so many other areas of social policy, the tax system is being used to meet an objective that would be better achieved through direct spending programs outside the tax system.

The disability tax credit

The disability tax credit is the single most important tax benefit for people with disabilities. Eligibility is based on a medical certificate filed along with the tax return.

Some disability groups, including the Coalition of Provincial Organizations for the Handicapped, support the credit because it provides a substantial benefit without the need for receipts. They have two major criticisms: the limited definition of disability in the program, and the fact that the credit is non-refundable.

Advocates believe that the non-refundability of the disability tax credit is its most important limitation. The average tax benefit in Ontario in 1990 was $751 per claimant – an amount that varied only slightly by income group. The fact that the disability tax credit is a tax relief measure and not a direct transfer means that the lowest-income group received the lowest benefit – on average $317. Some individuals receive nothing despite having significant disability-related expenses.

However, if a person has a spouse or supporting relative with a taxable income high enough to use all or part of the unused portion, the family unit can still benefit because the disability tax credit is transferable. In 1990, 30 per cent of disability tax credit claims were transferred to other taxpayers.

Transferability significantly reduces the losses to low-income people with disabilities. But there remains an inequity between disabled persons with supporting relatives and those without. Transferability is also perceived to reinforce the dependency of people with disabilities. A refundable credit has the advantage of being paid directly to the person with the disability.

In principle, we support the extension of the support provided now by the disability tax credit to non–tax-paying individuals with disabilities. The disability tax credit is clearly a social benefit that bears no relationship to the actual spending of individuals on disability-related needs or to the degree of their disabilities. It reflects the government's desire to provide a general benefit to all people with severe disabilities and should be designed to do that. However, we do not

believe that the appropriate response is to make the credit refundable.

If Ontario gains control over the non-refundable tax credits in its income tax, we recommend that the disability tax credit be converted to a flat rate benefit delivered outside the tax system. Government should provide, as a matter of social commitment, a constant dollar benefit, regardless of income, to all eligible people with disabilities. Such a program would have the advantage over the tax credit system of being administered by the appropriate government department responsible for support for people with disabilities, rather than federal or provincial departments of finance that have little experience with such matters.

Medical expenses tax credit and attendant care deduction

The medical expenses tax credit provides a non-refundable credit for medical expenses above a threshold of 3 per cent of net income. In addition, an employed person can deduct part-time attendant care costs up to a maximum of $5000 from income.

People with disabilities express several criticisms of the medical expenses tax credit. These criticisms concern the expenses threshold, the limited list of allowed expenses, the fact that the credit is not refundable, and the design of the special deduction for part-time attendant care costs.

> *"I've sat in this wheelchair for 30 years and every year I have to go back to the doctor to verify that I'm a paraplegic."*
> *~ Hearings participant, Disabled Alliance Network, Thunder Bay*

The threshold allows people who incur substantial costs in one tax year as a result of sickness or temporary disability to receive a greater subsidy than those with chronic disabilities who incur lower annual costs, but on an ongoing basis. People with disabilities are also frustrated that self-employed persons with disabilities seem to be able to claim disability-related expenses as business expenses with no threshold.

Critics also argue that the list of goods and services that can be claimed is too restrictive. An estimated 45 per cent of the disability-related expenses of those with severe disabilities are not itemized as eligible under the credit. The fact that the credit is non-refundable raises the same issues as the disability credit.

The treatment of attendant care expenses has been criticized because of its bias against the generally less costly and more desirable option of independent living at home. Disabled individuals who live in nursing homes or other institutions can claim the entire cost of their care as a medical expense, while those who live at home and participate in day programs or have attendant care are limited to a $5000 deduction. This deduction is extremely complex. At present, many claimants are forced to seek professional tax advice and planning to ensure they benefit from available tax options. In addition, as a deduction this provision is more valuable for those earning higher incomes and paying taxes at higher marginal rates.

If the Tax Collection Agreements are amended to permit provincial governments to determine their own income tax expenditures, we recommend that Ontario eliminate both the medical expenses tax credit and the deduction for attendant care. A program should be established outside the tax system to reimburse people with disabilities for a percentage of the costs related to their disabilities.

Seniors and taxes

The age credit
The federal Old Age Security program is no longer a universal benefit because it is taxed back from seniors with higher incomes. As a result, the age credit, available to all individuals aged 65 or older, is the only fiscal measure left in Canada that delivers a public benefit to seniors at all income levels.

In principle, we support the idea of a public benefit for seniors delivered through the tax system. However, we believe that such a benefit should be provided to all low-income seniors, not just seniors with taxable income. For this reason, if the Tax Collection Agreements are amended to permit provincial governments to determine the value of their own non-refundable tax credits, we recommend that Ontario eliminate the age credit in favour of a seniors tax credit, which should be refundable and income-tested based on family income.

The pension income credit
Seniors who receive private pension benefits or annuity income may claim a credit of 17 per cent of the first $1000 of income received from that pension in computing their Basic Federal Tax. At the current provincial tax rate of 58 per cent of Basic Federal Tax, this generates a further benefit of 9.9 per cent of the first $1000 against provincial tax.

The tax benefit provided by the pension income credit is equal to approximately $270 in tax relief for seniors at all income levels if they have incomes high enough to pay taxes. The average tax benefit in 1990 was $233.

However, the average benefit for tax filers with incomes below $10,000 was just $83, largely because only a small proportion of these individuals had qualifying income. Over 65 per cent of those who claimed the pension income credit had incomes below

$30,000. Any unused portion of the credit is transferable to a tax-paying spouse. In 1990 the total federal and provincial tax expenditure in Ontario for the credit was $172 million. Ontario's share was $58 million.

The major explanation for this skewed pattern of benefits is that the credit is only available for income from private pension plans. Pension income from public plans like Old Age Security and the Canada Pension Plan does not qualify.

In addition, there is an inherent bias against women in this provision because women are far less likely than men to have a private pension or annuity income.

We can see no justification for providing an additional tax subsidy to seniors who have private pension income. If provincial governments gain more control over their personal income tax through amendments to the federal-provincial Tax Collection Agreements, we recommend that Ontario eliminate the pension income credit. The revenue recovered by eliminating this credit should be used to increase the value of our proposed seniors tax credit.

Retirement savings

While public pension programs available to all Canadians are being cut back, tax assistance to private retirement savings, which is disproportionately of benefit to higher-income individuals, has been increased.

The national total tax expenditure for the deduction of contributions to Registered Retirement Savings Plans (RRSPs) and registered pension plans (RPPs) and the non-taxation of interest accruals was estimated to be $15.4 billion in 1989. The total provincial tax expenditure in Ontario was $2.7 billion.

Only a small part of the revenue forgone was recovered through taxation of withdrawals from these plans. At the federal level, $3.5 billion in tax was collected from withdrawals in 1989; Ontario's share of the tax receipts on withdrawal was $720 million. The provincial tax expenditure for retirement income savings in Ontario, after the taxes on withdrawals are taken into account, was $1.98 billion in 1989.

These tax expenditures are extremely costly in forgone revenue and are equivalent to almost 42 per cent of total government direct spending on retirement income through such programs as OAS and CPP.

Higher contribution limits for pension plans and RRSPs are being phased in and will result in even greater revenue losses over the next few years.

"Older women who have been full-time homemakers and find themselves divorced are falling between the cracks. We're simply left out in the cold in our retirement years."
~ Hearings participant, Mississauga

The coverage of the system is limited, particularly among women. Only 50 per cent of men and 39 per cent of women in employment have private pension plans. For RRSPs, the figures are 27 per cent of men and 19 per cent of women. Given the likely double counting in these two sets of figures – arising from the fact that many people both belong to private pension plans and contribute to RRSPs – the data suggest that a significant proportion of the population gains no benefit from this system. In addition, the system is designed so that the higher the taxpayer's income, the bigger the tax subsidy. The limits on tax-assisted retirement saving are tied directly to earned income, up to a maximum amount of tax-free saving.

And, because the assistance is in the form of a deduction from income, the tax benefit flowing from a given dollar amount of retirement savings increases as the marginal rate of tax paid by the taxpayer increases.

Social Policy Issues

The average tax benefit of the RRSP deduction of contributions was $1079 per claimant in 1990. It was $3663 for those with incomes above $150,000 and less than $1000 for those with incomes under $40,000.

With the significant increase in the maximum RRSP contribution since 1989, this disparity has almost certainly grown. Not surprisingly, a significant number of high-income tax filers take advantage of the benefit, compared with taxpayers at lower income levels.

"The current RRSP structure allows for tax-assisted savings that result in a net income much higher than average workers' earnings... we are subsidizing the wrong income groups."
~ Ontario Public Service Employees Union, Toronto hearing

The tax treatment of retirement savings can be seen as one way for people to spread their income over a longer period of time for tax purposes, making their tax liability better reflect their income over the long term. Nevertheless, because the principal public policy rationale for providing special tax treatment for retirement savings has always been to encourage Canadians to save for their retirement, we believe the program should be judged on that basis.

Assuming that the objective of public policy for retirement income is to ensure that all Canadians have adequate incomes in retirement, we believe that some adjustment should be made to achieve a fairer balance between public support for private retirement savings delivered through the tax system and other forms of public support for retirement.

We see no justification for subsidizing individuals who are members of registered pension plans or who contribute to RRSPs to accumulate pensions equivalent to 2.5 times the average industrial wage, when other forms of public assistance to retirement savings, such as OAS and CPP, provide benefits which are capped at much lower levels.

We recommend that Ontario seek the cooperation of the federal government to reduce the maximum retirement benefit eligible for tax assistance through the deduction for contributions to pension plans and RRSPs in the personal income tax and the deduction for contributions in the corporate income tax to 1.5 times the average industrial wage from the current 2.5.

For anyone with an income below $50,100 in 1993 (1.5 times the average industrial wage), our recommendations would have no impact on the tax assistance available.

This lower limit should be phased in by freezing the pension maximum and corresponding contribution limits at current levels until the maximum pension and corresponding limits are equivalent to 1.5 times the average industrial wage. Thereafter, contribution limits should be indexed to maintain the ratio.

We also do not believe that tax assistance to private retirement savings should provide greater relative support to higher-income earners than to lower-income earners for the same dollar amount of retirement savings.

We recommend that Ontario seek the agreement of the federal government to convert the deductions for contributions to registered pension plans and RRSPs in the personal income tax and corporate income tax to tax credits. Withdrawals from plans would continue to be taxed as ordinary income.

Social Policy Issues

MAKING THE TAX SYSTEM MORE PROGRESSIVE

 ## The basis for progressive taxation

In our discussion of taxation based on ability to pay, we identified two general types of arguments for progressive taxation. One is related to equal marginal sacrifice: the idea that a fair tax system should require taxpayers to make equivalent sacrifices of well-being when they pay taxes according to increases in the economic resources at their disposal. The other is based on principles of distributive justice, which suggest that the tax system should be used to effect a more equal distribution of income and wealth in our society. As we point out in our discussion of tax fairness, it is impossible to distinguish between those elements of the tax system whose purpose is to achieve a progressive tax system on tax fairness grounds and those whose purpose is to redistribute income or wealth. However, the factual starting points for arguments for change based on these propositions are different.

In arguing for a more progressive tax system on tax fairness grounds, we look at the burden of taxation faced by families at different income levels. We find that the overall burden of taxes in Ontario is roughly proportional. Taxes on average make up roughly the same proportion of household income as household income increases.

The finding that the tax system is not progressive overall also suggests that there is little redistribution of economic resources taking place through the tax system.

Whether or not that is a problem depends on two things: how income and wealth are currently distributed in Ontario; and what our goals as a society are for the distribution of economic resources among the population.

How income and wealth are distributed

Both income and wealth are distributed unequally in Ontario, although the distribution of wealth is far more unequal than the distribution of income. In 1991, the lowest-income 20 per cent of households received less than 5 per cent of the total income in Ontario. The highest-income 20 per cent of households received about 43 per cent of total income.

> *"The unequal distribution of wealth, property and power demonstrates the 'savage inequalities' in this country ..."*
> *~ Hearings participant, Thunder Bay*

The distribution of income among households has become more unequal over the last 20 years (1971 to 1991). The proportion of total income received by the lowest-income 10 per cent of families (those with incomes under $12,952) and of

More Progressive System

FIGURE 4
HOW INCOME IS DIVIDED FOR
FAMILIES AND UNATTACHED
INDIVIDUALS, ONTARIO

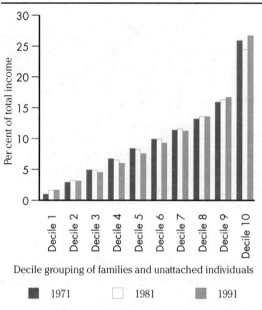

Decile grouping of families and unattached individuals

■ 1971   □ 1981   ▨ 1991

Source: Statistics Canada, Household Surveys Division,
Survey of Consumer Finances, unpublished data.

unattached individuals has increased only slightly from 1 per cent of total income to about 1 1/2 per cent. The proportion of income received by middle-income earners has declined.The proportion of total income received by the highest income earners has increased.

The distribution of wealth, the market value of assets minus liabilities at a given point in time, tends to be even more unequal than the distribution of income. In 1989 the wealthiest 20 per cent of households held 74 per cent of household wealth, while the 20 per cent of households with the highest pre-tax income received 43 per cent of income in the province. Even more striking, the wealthiest 5 per cent of households held 46 per cent of household wealth in the province, and the wealthiest 1 per cent of households held about 23 per cent of household wealth.

FIGURE 5
HOW WEALTH IS DIVIDED: DISTRIBUTION OF HOUSEHOLD WEALTH IN ONTARIO, 1989

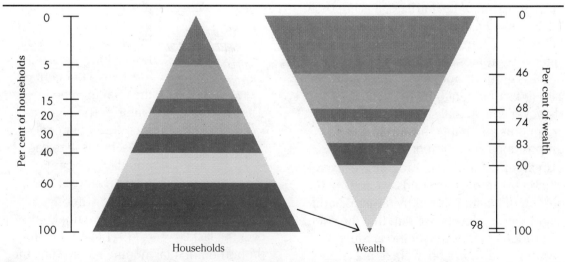

Source: Fair Tax Commission calculations based on Ernst & Young, *The Wealth Report* (Toronto, 1990), vol. 2, app. N.
Note: The definition of household in the Ernst & Young study includes all persons – even if unrelated – who share a common dwelling.

TABLE 2
SOURCES OF TAXABLE INCOME BY INCOME GROUP (INDIVIDUALS), ONTARIO, 1989

	Income group ($ thousands)						
	10 and under	10–30	30–60	60–100	100–250	Over 250	All tax filers
Distribution of tax filers (%)	27.1	40.7	26.1	4.4	1.4	0.3	100.0
Distribution of income by income group (%)							
Employment income	3.7	28.3	45.7	12.1	5.0	5.4	100.0
Taxable transfers (e.g., UI)	20.0	55.6	19.5	3.3	1.2	0.3	100.0
Pensions and annuities	7.4	47.6	32.1	8.5	3.2	1.1	100.0
Taxable dividends	0.5	9.6	21.9	17.9	21.9	28.1	100.0
Taxable capital gains	0.6	3.7	12.0	16.8	25.2	41.8	100.0
Other investment income	6.2	33.6	29.9	11.9	9.3	9.0	100.0
Net self-employment income	4.5	20.0	19.2	13.1	28.7	14.4	100.0
Miscellaneous	10.9	30.3	25.1	10.5	9.2	14.0	100.0
Total	4.6	29.3	39.7	11.8	7.2	7.4	100.0
Composition of income by income source (%)							
Employment income	56.9	69.4	82.7	73.3	49.2	52.5	71.9
Taxable transfers (e.g., UI)	15.0	6.6	1.7	1.0	0.6	0.1	3.5
Pensions and annuities	10.1	10.2	5.1	4.5	2.8	1.0	6.3
Taxable dividends	0.3	0.7	1.2	3.4	6.8	8.5	2.2
Taxable capital gains	0.4	0.4	0.9	4.3	10.7	17.4	3.1
Other investment income	9.1	7.8	5.1	6.8	8.7	8.2	6.8
Net self-employment income	4.8	3.3	2.4	5.4	19.4	9.5	4.9
Miscellaneous	3.4	1.5	0.9	1.3	1.8	2.8	1.5
Total	100.0	100.0	100.0	100.0	100.0	100.0	100.0

Source: Fair Tax Commission calculations based on Revenue Canada microdata file.
Note: Numbers may not add to 100 per cent due to rounding.

Options for a more progressive tax system

As we noted in our discussion of tax fairness, one of the ways to make the tax system more progressive is to make individual elements more progressive. We therefore focus on three key issues: the tax treatment of sources of income that are disproportionately attributed to higher-income individuals; the income tax rate schedule; and the taxation of wealth.

Taxation of dividends and capital gains

Both dividend and capital gains income from Canadian corporate shares receive special treatment.

Table 2 presents information on the types of income earned by different income groups in Ontario for the taxation year 1989. The top portion of the table shows the percentage of all income and of each source of income received by each income group. The bottom portion indicates the composition of income for all tax filers in aggregate and within each income group.

Two patterns are clearly apparent in the data on dividends and capital gains. First, from the top portion of the table, the distribution of different sources of income by income group indicates that, of the total amount of dividends and capital gains received by Ontario tax filers in 1989, most were received by high-income tax filers with taxable incomes of $100,000 or more:

21.9 per cent of the taxable amount of Canadian dividends and 25.2 per cent of taxable capital gains were received by tax-payers with incomes of $100,000 to $250,000; and 28.1 per cent of dividends and 41.8 per cent of capital gains were received by taxpayers with incomes greater than $250,000.

Second, as shown in the bottom part of the table, statistics on the composition of income within each income group indicate that dividends and capital gains accounted for a much larger share of total income for high-income tax filers with taxable incomes over $100,000 in 1989 than they did for all other tax filers. Dividends accounted for 2.2 per cent of all taxable income in Ontario in 1989 and capital gains accounted for 3.1 per cent, but tax filers in the $100,000 to $250,000 income group received 6.8 per cent of their total income in the form of dividends from Canadian corporate shares and 10.7 per cent in the form of capital gains; tax filers with taxable incomes above $250,000 received 8.5 per cent from dividends and 17.4 per cent from capital gains.

In our view, two important points emerge from these statistics. First, to the extent that these kinds of income receive favourable treatment under the current tax system, the benefits accrue mainly to taxpayers with taxable incomes of $100,000 or more.

Second, since dividends and capital gains make up a much larger share of income received by these tax filers than they do for others, measures to reduce or eliminate any preferences can be expected to enhance the progressivity of the income tax and the tax system as a whole, even if the schedule of rates remains unchanged.

The dividend tax credit

In determining the tax payable on dividend income from Canadian corporations, the taxable amount of dividends is calculated by adding 25 per cent to the cash value of dividends actually received. This theoretically makes the increased amount equal to the before-tax income originally earned by the corporation. A federal dividend tax credit is then provided in an amount equal to two-thirds of this 25 per cent "gross-up." Subsequently, a taxpayer is subject to tax on the net amount of the original dividend less the dividend tax credit.

This produces roughly the same tax result as if the individual had earned the income directly. The tax system avoids imposing a tax penalty for incorporation by ensuring that income earned through a corporation is not subject to tax twice – once at the corporate level and again at the personal level.

There are two key arguments advanced for the dividend tax credit. One is that it enhances the fairness of the tax system by eliminating the double taxation that would result if the corporate and personal income tax systems were treated as entirely separate. The other is that it is a necessary incentive for Canadians to invest in the shares of Canadian corporations.

We believe the dividend tax credit is defective as a mechanism for integrating the corporate and personal income taxes, for three reasons.

First, the dividend tax credit is available only to Canadian shareholders of taxable Canadian corporations.

Second, the dividend tax credit is not available to tax-exempt shareholders such as charitable organizations and pension plans.

Third, the gross-up and credit apply at fixed rates, regardless of the amount of income tax paid by the corporation.

Our assessment of these defects led us to conclude that the dividend tax credit functions as an incentive to encourage

Canadian ownership of Canadian corporations more than it does as an effective method of integration.

This in turn suggests that the dividend tax credit should be evaluated on the same basis as any other tax expenditure, by asking whether the incentive is an effective way to achieve the desired policy objective and whether it is consistent with other goals of the tax system – in particular, that of fairness.

The argument for the dividend tax credit as an investment incentive is that it encourages equity investment in Canadian companies and lowers the cost of capital to Canadian firms. However, this argument overlooks the increasing international integration of capital markets that makes it possible for Canadian businesses (especially large companies) to obtain equity capital throughout the world.

In fact, since international integration of capital markets implies that the cost of equity capital is determined mainly by the international marketplace, the ultimate effect of the dividend tax credit is to increase Canadian ownership of Canadian corporations and to reduce foreign investment in these corporations. While the dividend tax credit may have produced a shift in investment between Canadian investors and foreign investors, its impact on total equity investment in Canadian corporations is likely to have been small.

Given its impact on the fairness of the tax system, its limitations as a mechanism for integrating corporate and personal income taxes, and its uncertain impact on investment in shares of Canadian corporations, we believe that it is time for a thorough reassessment of the role of the dividend tax credit in the Canadian tax structure.

It is essential, however, that this review be done jointly by the federal and provincial governments. Measures to restructure the current gross-up and credit mechanism cannot realistically be undertaken by a single province acting alone. Income is often earned in several provinces (and allocated among them on the basis of a formula), and dividends are frequently paid by corporations resident in one or more provinces to shareholders resident in other provinces.

We recommend that Ontario discuss with the federal government the effectiveness of the dividend tax credit with a view to either eliminating it or restructuring it. This would require appropriate measures to ensure that small business income is subject to the same amount of tax whether it is earned directly through self-employment or a partnership, or indirectly through a Canadian-controlled private corporation.

Capital gains

Capital gains also benefit from special treatment in the personal income tax. Gains are recognized for tax purposes on realization (or deemed realization, for example, at death) rather than as they accrue; one-quarter of gains are excluded for tax purposes; and taxpayers are granted lifetime exemptions of $100,000 or, if the gain is from the sale of a farm or assets of a small business, of $500,000.

In 1991, the exclusion of 25 per cent of capital gains reduced provincial personal income tax revenue by $267 million and corporate tax revenue by $300 million; the general lifetime exemptions of $100,000 and the special $500,000 exemption for gains on small business and farming assets cost $529 million in forgone revenue.

Because tax may be deferred until capital gains are realized, it can also be argued that this type of capital income is treated more favourably than other kinds of income on

More
Progressive
System

which tax must be paid each year. In addition, capital gains may benefit from a further tax advantage in that taxpayers can minimize tax by choosing to realize gains when other income is low (in order to benefit from lower marginal tax rates).

THE CAPITAL GAINS EXCLUSION

Several justifications have been advanced for the 25 per cent exclusion.

First, it is often argued that the exclusion is a "rough justice" compensation for inflation. The tax system taxes nominal capital gains, only a portion of which reflects real gains; the remainder simply maintains the real value of the capital asset in the face of inflation. In a fair tax system, only real gains should be taxed. On this argument, the 25 per cent exclusion can be regarded as a way to limit tax to real gains, if only approximately.

Second, it is sometimes defended on the basis that it offsets the incentive created by gains taxation to retain assets to avoid incurring tax – sometimes referred to as the "lock-in problem."

Third, for corporate shares that appreciate in value when tax-paid earnings are retained at the corporate level, the exclusion can be viewed as an arrangement to integrate the corporate and personal income taxes and to prevent double taxation of income earned through a corporation.

Finally, the exclusion is sometimes treated as an incentive to increase investment.

If the exclusion is a rough justice adjustment for inflation, it would appear to be too rough to constitute justice. The 25 per cent exclusion is fixed; it is not dependent on how long an individual holds an asset or on the rate of inflation in the period over which the asset is held. In recent years we have seen the inclusion rate rise in stages from 50 per cent to 75 per cent in a

manner that bears little if any relation to inflation rates. In addition, since allowable interest deductions are based on nominal rather than real interest costs, a partial inflation allowance is already built into the system. Clearly, if an inflation adjustment is thought to be necessary, an index adjustment is preferable. This, in fact, is what several countries now do, including Australia and the United Kingdom.

The exclusion is also too blunt to serve as an antidote for the lock-in problem. The impact of locking in depends on how long an asset has been held, and the difference between the taxes payable on its sale and those that would have been payable if the gain had been taxed on an accrual basis. In any event, in Canada this problem is substantially reduced by the requirement (subject to various exceptions) that capital gains tax is payable when property is transferred by gift or at death.

If the exclusion of capital gains from full taxation is viewed as a mechanism to prevent double taxation of income earned through a corporation, it is poorly designed for this purpose as well. On this justification there would be no reason for the exclusion to apply to assets other than corporate shares. Furthermore, like the dividend tax credit, the capital gains exclusion applies regardless of how much income tax was actually paid by the corporation. It is of questionable value for large corporations that are able to obtain equity capital throughout the world.

Finally, as an investment incentive, the capital gains exclusion is poorly targeted. Presumably one would want to encourage productive investment in Canada. As with the dividend tax credit, the predominant result may be the displacement of foreign direct investment with Canadian investment. In addition, the exclusion applies to

More Progressive System

all capital gains, not only to those earned on Canadian investments. The incentive effect is also provided only when a successful investment is liquidated, not when the investment is actually made.

Although we oppose the continuation of the 25 per cent exclusion for capital gains, we have concluded that it is impossible for Ontario alone to tax capital gains at the regular personal and corporate income tax rates for two reasons. First, Ontario residents could easily avoid this measure by transferring appreciated property into a corporation resident in another province (since this is allowed on a tax-deferred basis), selling the property in the other province, and paying themselves a tax-preferred capital dividend. Second, to the extent that the exclusion functions like the dividend tax credit to reduce the combined burden on income earned at the corporate level, initiatives by a single province acting alone have to be ruled out. Since corporate income is often earned in several provinces, and shares can be held and traded in any of the provinces, such a system would be administratively impossible.

THE CAPITAL GAINS EXEMPTIONS

Unlike the 25 per cent exclusion, which is at least partially justified in tax design terms, the lifetime exemptions were introduced and justified as tax expenditures. They were to provide an incentive for investment and risk taking in general, with special assistance for farms and small businesses. They are also intended to compensate for the difficulties farmers and small business owners encounter in obtaining access to credit.

In our view, the exemption is too poorly targeted in terms of both focus and timing to achieve its stated purposes effectively. Its

continuation cannot be justified given the measure of tax fairness sacrificed. If governments wish to provide incentives for investment and risk-taking to enhance economic growth, measures that are more directly focused would be preferable. An investment subsidy provided through the capital gains exemption does not direct investment to activities or sectors that one might identify in an economic development strategy. Rather, it offers the same benefits for capital gains from a wide array of investments, including those made outside the country, regardless of their economic impact.

The timing of the benefit is also questionable. Although knowledge that realized capital gains will ultimately be exempt does provide some incentive, a much more effective incentive would be one that subsidizes investors at the time an investment is being made. Further, risk taking would be encouraged more effectively by some mechanism to address investment losses rather than through the existing mechanism that rewards winners after the fact. Moreover, tax breaks at the "back-end" of the investment cycle do not address the problem of access to capital or credit; they only benefit those who have, at least to some extent, already solved that problem.

The exemption for farms is often defended on the grounds that it operates as a form of pension fund and that it supports the survival of family farms in Canada. The pension element of farm capital would be better and more fairly addressed by creating closer parallels between this form of investment and more conventional pension funds. For example, on the sale of a farm, some portion of the proceeds could be deposited in a Registered Retirement Savings Plan. They would then be taxed as they are withdrawn and consumed in the same way that other pensions and retire-

More Progressive System

ment funds are taxed. The maintenance of family farms is addressed by other provisions, including the "rollover" provision that permits the transfer of a farm to the owner's children by gift or at death without tax.

We find the arguments for the lifetime capital gains exemptions not strong enough to justify the tax fairness sacrificed, and on that basis we conclude that they should be abolished. Action by the federal government that would affect the federal and provincial income tax would be preferable.

However, since the exemption (unlike the exclusion) operates only in the personal income tax and is not linked with the dividend tax credit, Ontario could reform its income tax in this area even without federal action. This could be accomplished under an amended tax collection agreement that allowed provinces to levy tax on taxable income and allowed the current capital gains exemption to be added back to "adjusted taxable income" for provincial taxation.

The income tax rate structure

The personal income tax rate structure is the most visible, though perhaps not the most important, way to achieve the desired relationship between income and the amount of tax paid. Often when people compare tax systems among jurisdictions, they compare statutory rate structures (as presented in the tax legislation), even though the ultimate effect of a tax results from the interaction of the rate and the base being taxed.

On several occasions during our public consultations we heard arguments for a "flat" tax. Generally, the flat tax idea is taken to mean that, after some basic income exemption, all income would be taxed at a single rate, and other deductions, exemptions, and credits would either be eliminated or strictly limited. It would be a simple

tax system and, because the base would be larger, the rate required to raise any level of revenue would be lower than the highest rates in a progressive schedule.

We are not convinced by these arguments. While a flat tax system would be simpler than the current income tax system (or one similarly structured), the cost in tax fairness far exceeds the benefits from simplicity. It would be impossible to achieve a degree of progressivity consistent with a fair income tax based on ability-to-pay principles.

"We view our farms as our retirement savings. This is not through choice, but of necessity. After operating and living expenses, any available money is usually invested in the farm, leaving nothing to purchase a retirement savings plan."
~ *Ontario Cattlemen's Association, Kenora hearing*

Accordingly, we adopt the position that the personal income tax should continue to be based on a progressive statutory rate structure, and that its progressivity should be strengthened.

We have three objectives in developing our recommendations on the rate structure for the personal income tax.

First, tax relief for individuals with low incomes should be strengthened. At present, many people in Ontario who live on family incomes below generally accepted measures of low income pay personal income tax. Our recommendations in this area deal with the establishment of a reformed tax credit system.

Second, we recommend that the degree of progressivity in the income tax structure be increased. The federal reforms of 1987–88 moved from 10 to three marginal rate brackets. As a result, individuals with considerable income differences pay tax at the same rate, and the top rate bracket is reached at the relatively modest taxable income of $59,180 (1993). The Ontario rates mirror the federal rates.

Third, we suggest that the top marginal rate not become excessively high. What is of concern here is the combined federal and provincial rates, because that is the marginal rate a taxpayer actually faces. While we are concerned that the top rate not be excessive, there is no clear guidance in the literature or elsewhere as to where this threshold lies. A popularly cited upper limit is 50 per cent, but there is really no special significance to this number.

While there is no obvious reason to choose one top marginal rate over another on tax fairness grounds, practical considerations may provide somewhat firmer guidance. For example, beyond some level, the effects of high tax rates may become strong enough to influence taxpayers' investment and work behaviour adversely. Further, in an open economy, investment in a "high tax" jurisdiction may decline in favour of "low tax" areas, and, ultimately, high-income individuals may relocate. Studies for the commission point to evidence supporting the effect of high levels, particularly in the location decisions for both investment and high-income individuals.

We also note that tension exists between our second and our third objectives. If one is concerned that the top marginal rate not become too high, the amount of progressivity that can be introduced into the rate schedule is limited.

If Ontario gains more control over its personal income tax system through amendments to the federal-provincial Tax Collection Agreements, we recommend that Ontario adopt a personal income tax rate schedule with the following features:

- A basic personal credit determined by multiplying the lowest Ontario personal income tax rate by the basic personal amount in the federal personal income tax.

- A rate schedule that is graduated over the middle-income range.

- A top marginal rate that would result in a combined federal/provincial top marginal rate of no more than 60 per cent, and which would apply to annual taxable income in excess of $250,000.

- No more than 10 tax brackets.

Wealth taxes

Taxes on wealth, either in the form of an annual net wealth tax or a wealth transfer tax, can enhance the progressivity of the overall tax system by addressing the limitations in the personal income tax as an adequate measure of people's ability to pay.

Because of publicity generated by the Wealth Tax Working Group's report and reports in the media about the provincial government's "plans" to impose wealth taxes, many people appeared at our public hearings to express their views.

While some urged the commission to consider wealth taxes as a means to improve the fairness of the tax system, others were strongly opposed to any form of wealth tax. Overall, public input revealed that many people were unsure about the structure and operation of wealth taxes, and about who would pay them.

There are two kinds of wealth taxes. An annual net wealth tax is a yearly tax on a household's accumulated assets minus its liabilities. A wealth transfer tax is a tax on transfers of wealth through gift or at the time of death. We examined both to evaluate their costs and benefits and to assess their viability at the provincial level.

The lessons of history

Today, Canada, Australia, and New Zealand are the only countries in the Organisation

More Progressive System

for Economic Co-operation and Development (OECD) that do not levy taxes on wealth. Every other country levies one or more of an annual tax on net wealth or a wealth transfer tax involving some combination of a gift tax, an inheritance tax (a tax on inheritors of wealth), and/or an estate tax (a tax on the estate of a deceased person).

Although annual net wealth taxes have never existed federally or provincially in Canada, wealth transfer taxes have a long history in this country. About 100 years ago, Ontario introduced a tax on wealth in the form of an inheritance tax.

In 1941 the federal government introduced a gift and estate tax, which continued until 1971. In 1979 Ontario abolished its succession duty, and in 1985 Quebec abolished the last provincial succession duty in Canada.

In principle, we believe that there is an important role for wealth taxation in the overall tax mix. Wealth taxes contribute to the fairness of the overall tax system in a variety of ways and can provide an important if secondary source of revenue. How practical it is to introduce a wealth tax, however, depends on the actual design of the tax and on whether it is enacted in Ontario or at the national level.

Wealth transfer tax vs. annual net wealth tax

Although we have strong reservations about the feasibility of an Ontario-only wealth transfer tax, we are firmly convinced that a national wealth transfer tax would be a practical and beneficial addition to the current tax mix in Canada.

A wealth transfer tax has several characteristics in its favour compared with an annual net wealth tax. Historically, Canadian taxation statistics indicate a progressive distribution of the wealth transfer

> *"We profess to believe in a society with equal opportunity for all and yet we continue to allow wealth to be passed from one generation to the next so that the person born into a wealthy family has considerable advantage over those born to poor families."*
> ~ Essex County Roman Catholic Separate School Board, Windsor hearing

tax burden, at least when measured against assessed net values of estates.

Available evidence also indicates that wealth transfer taxes can make a meaningful contribution to government revenues. Ontario raised over $60 million from its gift tax and succession duty in 1975–76. Estimates of actual wealth transfer tax revenues raised in OECD member countries as a percentage of gross domestic product suggest that revenues from a Canada-wide wealth transfer tax are most likely to be in the range of $1.7 billion to $2.1 billion (0.29 per cent of GDP, as in the United States). Since Ontario households hold roughly 45 per cent of Canadian household net wealth, the share for Ontario revenues from such a tax is likely be in the range of $765 million to $945 million. Although wealth transfer tax revenues are likely to be similar to those that might be obtained from an annual net wealth tax, the administrative costs of a wealth transfer tax would almost certainly be lower.

First, the number of taxpayers that would be subject to a wealth transfer tax in any year is only a fraction of the number that would have to pay an annual net wealth tax. There were almost 215,000 Ontario households with net wealth of more than $1 million in 1989. A study conducted for the commission estimates that among residents of Ontario who died in 1989 there were only 2500 estates valued at more than $1 million.

Second, unlike an annual net wealth tax, which would have to rely on costly annual valuations or valuation rules that facilitate the administration of the tax but undermine its fairness and efficiency, a wealth transfer tax could be based on valuations that are already required for purposes of capital gains tax on deemed dispositions (for property that has increased in value) or probate fees (for property subject to probate at death).

More generally, because wealth transfer taxes have a long history in Canada, it might be expected that taxpayers and collection authorities would face fewer initial costs with this kind of wealth tax than with an annual net wealth tax, with which Canada has little or no experience.

> *"There is no reason why income from an inheritance should be treated differently from earned income – such a tax is necessary to fill the gaps in the taxation of wealthy individuals that cannot reasonably be addressed through changes to the income tax system."*
> *~ Toronto Association of Neighbourhood Services, Toronto hearing*

Finally, the economic impact of a wealth transfer tax is less worrisome than that of an annual net wealth tax, which may discourage saving regardless of its purpose. Wealth transfer taxes should affect only savings for the purpose of transferring wealth.

On balance, we believe that an annual net wealth tax is neither practical nor feasible at the provincial level. Although such a tax would enhance the fairness of the tax system as a whole, its revenue potential is too uncertain, its administrative costs too great, and its economic implications too troubling to warrant its introduction.

Can Ontario go it alone?

Whether it would be feasible for Ontario to levy a wealth transfer tax if it were the only province to do so is much less certain. Based on experiences in Canada and Australia, where subnational wealth transfer taxes were abandoned after the national government withdrew from this tax field, it might be reasonable to conclude that these taxes are sustainable only at the national level.

Probably more significant than the administrative and constitutional obstacles, a provincial wealth transfer tax would be extremely vulnerable to location decisions that might substantially reduce revenues raised and affect the general level of economic activity in the province. To the extent that the tax applied to the estates of donors resident in Ontario at death, people could avoid the tax by moving to another province upon retirement.

Alternatively, although tax might still be imposed on transfers of property situated in Ontario and on receipts by resident beneficiaries, the former could be avoided by transferring property to a corporation resident in another province while the latter could be avoided through the use of planning devices like trusts or evaded by failing to report property received from outside the province.

Although relocation and tax planning are by no means without cost, they are much less costly within a country than they are between countries.

Further, although the studies reviewed suggest that the impact of taxes on business and personal location decisions is generally less important than other non-tax considerations, the potential savings from avoiding a wealth transfer tax may be substantial. It is reasonable to expect that persons with large estates would not willingly endure a tax they need not pay in any other province, but would move to avoid the tax.

More Progressive System

TABLE 3
ESTIMATED DISTRIBUTIVE IMPACT AND REVENUE POTENTIAL FROM A
COMPREHENSIVE ESTATE TAX IN ONTARIO

| Estate size ($ millions) | Taxable estates | | Average tax paid by | | | | Revenue raised ($ millions) |
| | | | Taxpaying estates | | All estates | | |
	#	% of all estates	$	Avg. % of estate	$	Avg. % of total value	
1.0–2.0	497	38.3	90,000	6.9	34,487	2.7	44.7
2.0–5.0	342	33.2	658,599	20.6	218,468	6.8	225.2
Over 5	85	44.5	4,339,137	28.1	1,931,029	12.5	368.8
All estates	924	1.6	691,339	20.9	10,840	3.6	638.8

Source: James B. Davies and David Duff, "Wealth Tax Proposals: Distributional Impact and Revenue Potential,"
in *Issues in the Taxation of Individuals*, ed. Allan M. Maslove, Fair Tax Commission Research Studies (Toronto:
University of Toronto Press, forthcoming).
Note: Exemption, $1 million; rate, 30% above $1 million; full exemption for transfers to surviving spouses.

A national wealth transfer tax

The revenue potential for Ontario from a national wealth transfer tax is substantial, and the distribution of such a tax would be highly progressive. A variety of simulation scenarios were prepared for the commission. To illustrate the potential impact of a tax on estates, one of these scenarios is presented in table 3. It models a tax with a 30 per cent rate applied to estates after allowing a $1 million general exemption and a complete exemption for transfers to surviving spouses. The revenue potential is estimated to be almost $640 million annually based on 1989 data. Over half the total would come from estates valued at over $5 million. They would be assessed an average tax of more than $4 million, compared with an average value of these estates of about $15 million.

We recommend a national wealth tax in the form of a wealth transfer tax as the preferred option. This kind of wealth tax is most familiar, administratively manageable, present in most developed countries, and most compatible with our views of fairness. This tax could be levied by the federal government or by all provinces acting together.

The base of the tax should be fully comprehensive (including principal residences, pension funds, and life insurance), the tax should apply to gifts as well as transfers at death, spousal transfers should be fully exempt, transfers should be taxable only on the portion of the transfer above a generous exemption, and there should be no credit for capital gains taxes on deemed dispositions. Estimates prepared for the commission suggest that a tax applied only to the value of estates in excess on one million dollars and exempted spousal transfers would apply to only 1.6 per cent of estates in Ontario.

If such a tax is introduced, and Ontario derives revenues from it, probate fees should be restructured so that they do not function as a progressive tax (as they do now), but as a user fee to reflect the true costs of processing wills.

THE TAX SYSTEM AND ECONOMIC ACTIVITY IN ONTARIO

All taxes affect economic activity in one way or another because they affect the decisions made by both businesses and individuals. Concerns related to the influence of taxation on the economic behaviour of individuals arise throughout our report. When we consider taxes paid by businesses, however, those concerns move to centre stage. First, the impact of taxes on corporate decision making was a prominent issue in our public consultation process in its own right. Second, because the fairness of corporate taxes depends on how the market ultimately distributes the tax burden among people, issues of economic impact are generally much more clearly defined in the taxation of corporations than issues of fairness.

We considered economic and fairness issues arising from corporate income and capital taxation, payroll taxation, and the taxation of small business and cooperatives. We also addressed the particular issues in mining and forestry taxation, where the objective is to recover for the public a fair share of the underlying value of resources held in common by the people of Ontario.

> *"In reality, corporations, including the much-maligned multinationals, are not faceless entities or owned by the cartoon image of a capitalist in striped trousers and top hat; anyone with savings in a mutual fund, pension or life insurance plan is a part owner."*
> *~ Submission, Burlington*

Corporate taxation in a fair tax system

Issues relating to corporate taxation were among the most contentious in our public hearings. For many participants, declining revenues from corporate income and capital taxation stood as a symbol of increasing unfairness in our overall tax system. For others, even our current levels of corporate taxation were cited as a major problem for Ontario as this province attempts to compete with jurisdictions with apparently lower corporate tax levels.

Our work in this area attempts both to focus the issues and to present information that may clarify these important questions. In the end, however, the facts and analysis can take us only so far. Jurisdictions are only beginning to address the financial and economic implications of the growing integration of the world economy over the past 25 years and the increased mobility of capital and economic activity.

At the same time, any discussion of changing the tax system must also consider who will actually pay the tax: corporate taxes tend to be passed on to employees in the form of lower wages, consumers in the form of higher prices, or investors in the form of lower dividends.

Economic Activity

Declining revenues

Canada is not alone in experiencing a declining share of revenues from corporate income taxation. The United States has experienced a similar decline.

One of the reasons revenue from taxes on corporate profits has declined relative to other underlying tax bases is that profitability reported by corporations has declined.

The long-term decline of corporate income tax as a share of provincial government revenue raises important questions of public policy.

- Are corporate tax rates lower than they should be in a fair system?
- What contribution would higher corporate tax revenue make to a fair tax system?

Competitiveness and rates in other jurisdictions

Ontario's corporate income tax rates are generally comparable to those of other provinces with the exception of Quebec. In 1993 the corporate income tax rate for manufacturing and processing profits, including both the federal and the provincial taxes, was 36.34 per cent in Ontario and 31.74 per cent in Quebec; the general rate was 44.34 per cent in Ontario and 37.74 per cent in Quebec. This disparity has led to tax-planning mechanisms that cause corporate income to be reported in Quebec. Quebec has higher payroll and capital tax rates, but these taxes are not directly relevant to the issue of income transfers.

Internationally, the principal point of comparison for Ontario's corporate tax rates is, of necessity, the United States, the predominant home country for foreign parents of Canadian subsidiaries. Prior to the federal tax reform in the two countries in the late 1980s, the Ontario and Canadian systems, with such features as the lower manufacturing and processing rate, were not at a disadvantage in terms of tax rates. This situation changed following tax reform; tax rates in the United States fell more than in Canada.

As a result of budgetary changes at the federal level and in Ontario in the last few years, manufacturing and processing profits are now taxed at a slightly lower rate in Canada than in the United States. For income not taxed at the manufacturing and processing rate, the rate in Ontario is higher than it is in the United States. However, the federal withholding tax on dividends paid to non-residents raises the effective tax rate on profits repatriated from Canadian subsidiaries to foreign parent corporations.

> "Government must ensure that its policies and programs do not place an unnecessary burden on the wealth-creating sectors – that the cost of programs do not exceed the benefits, and that the programs themselves do not impede growth."
> ~ Ontario Forest Industries Association, Toronto hearing

Corporate taxation and economic behaviour

Opinion is sharply divided on the issue of the impact of tax differences on the location of economic activity. However, most commentators would agree that other economic factors will be the dominant consideration in most location decisions. At the same time, it is important to note that competing jurisdictions have tended to keep their tax systems within narrow ranges of tax rates and incentives for investment.

Although the evidence regarding the effect of corporate taxes on business location decisions is not conclusive, there is reason to believe that tax rates have some effect on where profits are declared. We

Economic Activity

agree that the role of other tax regimes in influencing what policy choices are appropriate for Ontario is going to be even more important in the future. It is critical that the nature of the constraints be fully appreciated. Tax levels that are significantly higher than those in competing jurisdictions will almost certainly have the paradoxical effect of lowering overall revenues by driving out the tax bases that are targeted for taxation.

Corporate tax rates

The corporate income tax base can move from province to province and country to country in response to statutory tax rate differentials. It is unlikely that revenue could be raised by increasing corporate income tax rates at this time.

We conclude that it would be counterproductive for the province to adopt corporate tax policies that depart significantly from those of other jurisdictions with which Ontario has a close economic relationship.

Ontario should maintain effective rates of tax on business at approximately their current levels relative to other jurisdictions, given the evidence with respect to:

- effective tax rates in competing jurisdictions;
- the impact of effective tax rates on business locations; and
- the fact that the burden of corporate taxes tends to be borne by employees, consumers, and investors.

An active response to limits on corporate taxes

If Ontario, other provinces, and other jurisdictions outside Canada are to maintain a fair level of taxation on income from capital, it will be necessary to coordinate tax policies much more effectively – both within Canada and internationally.

Ontario should seek agreements with the federal and provincial governments to minimize interprovincial tax competition. Agreements should provide for such measures as:

- consolidated taxation in which the tax-paying unit would include all the Canadian members of a corporate group; and
- minimum provincial corporate tax rates.

National jurisdictions also face constraints in their ability to tax the income of multinational corporations. In addition to respecting those constraints in establishing its own policy, Ontario should urge the federal government to play an active role in promoting initiatives such as international tax agreements to ensure that the income of multinational corporations is taxed fairly.

Tax expenditures and corporate minimum taxes

Popular criticism of the corporate tax system has often pointed to profitable corporations that pay little or no corporate tax. This situation is perceived to be primary evidence of problems with the current tax structure, particularly in three basic areas.

First, it is seen as inappropriate that corporations with profitable operations in the province benefit from government services without supporting such services through income tax.

Second, the ability of corporations to make profits and to distribute income without tax is seen as a significant fairness issue. This concern is amplified because the dividends received at the individual level are then taxed at preferential rates, as a result of the dividend tax credit.

Third, untaxed profit is seen as a potential tax base, which could yield substantial tax revenues and check the slide of corporate tax revenues as a share of provincial revenue.

The report of the Corporate Minimum Tax Working Group analysed the reasons why some corporations paid no corporate income tax. Of the 23,300 profitable corporations that paid no Ontario income tax in 1989, roughly 12,800 were non-taxable because of a since-abolished tax holiday Ontario offered new small businesses in 1989; 1600 paid no corporate income tax in Ontario because, to prevent double taxation of income earned in the corporate sector, inter-corporate dividends are not taxed; 2200 used prior years' losses to offset corporate income tax otherwise payable; and a further 6700 (with total book profits of almost $6 billion, $3.3 billion of which were allocated to Ontario for tax purposes) were non-taxable for other reasons. Of this $3.3 billion, 65 per cent was not taxable because of major tax expenditures including the capital cost allowance (41 per cent); the resource deduction (11 per cent); the capital gains exclusion (8 per cent); and the Research and Development Super Allowance (5 per cent).

When the federal government introduced its tax reforms in 1987, one of the objectives was to reduce the number of profitable corporations escaping tax altogether. These reforms also affect Ontario, because almost all the federal changes were also adopted in this province.

The data for 1989 do not fully reflect the effect of tax reform, since many changes were phased in over a number of years. Other changes will have their full impact only after assets that were in place before tax reform have been replaced; for example, reduced rates of tax depreciation apply only to assets purchased after reform. The possibility exists that the 1989 information on profitable, non–tax-paying

firms may overstate the issue. Nevertheless, the large pool of losses and carried-over deductions that existed at the time of reform, the incentives that still remain in place, and the losses associated with the serious recession of the last few years all suggest that the phenomenon of profitable, non–tax-paying corporations is likely to continue at least for some time.

This situation is a direct consequence of the fact that, through tax expenditures, significant subsidies are delivered to corporations through the tax system. When those subsidies are claimed by a profitable corporation and exceed the amount of tax that would otherwise be payable by the corporation based on its income, the result is a profitable corporation that appears to pay no income tax.

In general, there are two potential responses to profitable corporations paying little or no corporate income tax as a result of the application of tax expenditures. One is to consider applying a special tax that would be imposed on profitable corporations that have been able to use subsidies delivered through the tax system to reduce their tax liability to zero. The other is to look at the underlying reasons for the phenomenon – the fact that subsidies to corporations are delivered through the tax system – and consider whether or not those subsidies are justifiable from a public policy perspective.

Corporate tax expenditures

If a tax expenditure is considered to be the most effective way to achieve a given public policy objective, the fact that a corporation may pay no tax as a result of having taken advantage of the provision cannot be seen, in and of itself, as evidence of a problem with the tax structure.

Although the specific public policy questions raised by individual subsidies go beyond our mandate into the realm of economic policy, we have addressed broader issues related to the process by which tax expenditures are devised, approved, administered, reviewed, and audited.

In addition to the criteria applicable to tax expenditures generally, those designed to further general economic development goals should meet the same criteria that apply to economic development programs delivered outside the tax system.

- Subsidies should be focused on desired activities or behaviours, not on sectors, types of companies, or size of businesses.

- The activities or behaviours targeted must be defined and measured easily.

- The incentives given should be large enough to result in changed corporate decisions.

- The subsidy programs must be simple to understand and transparent for both companies and the administrative authorities.

- Before they are introduced, all subsidy programs should be reviewed in depth with potential recipient firms for their likely impact on behaviour.

Tax expenditures to support economic activity have the twin characteristics of not being highly visible to the general population and yet being very visible to their targeted beneficiaries. The combination of these two attributes makes them hard to modify as the economic objectives of government evolve. A more general difficulty in using the tax system as an instrument of economic policy is that there is no recognized set of criteria by which tax incentives are created and evaluated.

Tax expenditures can also be potentially costly to the government if significant resources are reallocated to the targeted low-tax activity. Often direct spending programs achieve greater success because they can be targeted and evaluated more easily. In addition, uncoordinated tax measures designed to achieve a variety of policy objectives can debilitate the tax system, making it less efficient, less equitable, and more complex.

Because tax incentives tend to operate at the margin, they are most effective if they are focused on making a particular type of activity significantly more attractive in Ontario than in comparable jurisdictions. Small tax advantages for Ontario in many areas will have less impact on corporate decision making than large differences in one or two key areas.

We conclude that, in general, the assistance Ontario offers through the tax system for business activity is too small to be meaningful relative to the values of other factors that affect business decisions. Although these incentives have a limited impact on corporate behaviour, they make the corporate tax system more complex – an effect that contributes to public perceptions about the unfairness of the corporate income tax.

We are also concerned about the pressure on provinces to compete for business investment by increasing tax expenditures and lowering statutory tax rates. If Ontario were to increase tax expenditures significantly for business activity in an effort to make more than a marginal impact on business decisions, this action could trigger interprovincial competition, bidding up of

> *"Tax expenditures can have positive socio-economic benefits. Many existing tax incentives perform useful social and economic functions ... However, they must be carefully targeted and their effectiveness monitored." ~ Submission, Ontario Natural Gas Association, Toronto*

Economic Activity

tax expenditures, and eroding corporate tax revenue. We conclude that Ontario should not try to modify or supplement tax-based subsidies to business in the federal tax system.

Corporate minimum tax

In the 1993 Ontario budget the government proposed a corporate minimum tax which would be based on income and in which the definition of corporate income for corporate minimum tax purposes would include the value of major tax expenditures claimed by the taxpayer.

Although we have considerable sympathy with the aim of this tax in attempting to deal with the problem of non–tax-paying and low–tax-paying profitable corporations, we are convinced that explicit recognition and a vigorous assessment of tax expenditures would address this issue more effectively than the application of a further corporate tax.

Taxation of the service industry

The preferential corporate income tax treatment of manufacturing and processing profits, compared with profits in all other sectors, is a fairness and competitiveness concern, given the growing role of the service sector in the Ontario economy.

In 1993 Ontario's general corporate income tax rate was 15.5 per cent, while the rate applied to the profits of manufacturing and processing firms was 13.5 per cent. The service sector, encompassing such activities as transportation, communications, personal and business services, tourism, and wholesale and retail trade, is taxed at the higher rate.

A number of economic factors combine to suggest we should reconsider this bias in favour of manufacturing. The nature of service industries has changed dramatical-

ly in recent years. They are now among the most technologically advanced and fastest changing industrial sectors. Service industries are also facing international competition to a much greater extent than has traditionally been the case.

Furthermore, the line between goods production and services production is becoming blurred. As a result, activities that contribute directly to the efficiency of manufacturing enterprises are often subject to the regular corporate tax rate.

Elimination of the manufacturing preference would also make the system much less complex, as it would no longer be necessary to make difficult distinctions between manufacturing and non-manufacturing activities in determining corporate tax liabilities.

We conclude that there is no longer a strong case for treating service and manufacturing income differently in the corporate tax system.

Payroll taxation

The Employer Health Tax (EHT) is the only payroll tax in Ontario's general revenue system (Workers' Compensation Board premiums are not part of the consolidated revenues of the provincial government). Although the tax took effect in 1990 – at the same time that the government eliminated premiums in the Ontario Health Insurance Plan – the name of the tax is misleading because it bears no relationship to provincial spending on health in Ontario.

Our review of the Employer Health Tax focuses on three aspects of payroll taxation in Ontario: the potential for payroll taxation to play a more significant role in the mix of taxes levied by Ontario; the graduated rate structure; and the proposal by the federal government to limit the deductibility of provincial payroll taxes from income for corporate income tax purposes.

Economic Activity

Should Ontario rely more on payroll taxes?

For several reasons, we were not persuaded that increased reliance on payroll taxes would be appropriate for Ontario at this time, despite the fact that these taxes are much higher in other jurisdictions.

A study done for the commission surveyed the many incidence studies on payroll taxes and concluded that "labour bears over 80 per cent of the employer payroll tax burden in the long-run"(Dahlby 1993, 133). To the extent that payroll taxes are borne by workers, there are alternative sources of revenue that result in a fairer distribution of the burden of taxation among the population as a whole.

In addition, we are concerned about evidence that employment would be reduced as a result of a payroll tax increase, even if such a reduction were only in the short term. With unemployment currently at unacceptably high levels and projected to stay at those levels for a number of years, and with structural changes in the economy making it difficult for older and less well-educated workers to find new jobs when they are laid off, we could not justify a recommendation that might put employment at risk.

> "High payroll taxes force small businesses to fire or not hire additional employees."
> ~ Chambre d'économique de l'Ontario, Toronto hearing

Impact on small business

Somewhat different issues surround the impact of payroll taxes on the small business sector. Small firms tend to be more labour intensive than large firms. For small firms, payroll costs tend to be a higher percentage of total expenses.

An increase in payroll taxation will be more significant for small firms on average than for large firms, because the initial impact will be to increase expenses by a proportionately greater amount. Even if the eventual result is that labour bears the tax, the transitional period may be more difficult for small business.

Graduated rate structure of the Employer Health Tax

The rate structure of the EHT leads to a number of undesirable results in the application of the tax. The rate structure adopted in 1990 was based on the desire to provide a preference for small business in the payroll tax replacing existing OHIP premiums. The preference was instituted by setting the rate for the smallest businesses, those with payrolls under $200,000, at half the rate for larger businesses.

OHIP premiums had been employer-paid to a much greater extent in large businesses than in small businesses. The split rate may have emerged as a "rough-justice" way to reduce the overall impact of the switch from the OHIP premium system to the payroll tax. While some people may argue that small business should benefit from a preferential rate of tax, there are both technical and policy reasons why this may not be desirable.

First, when an employer moves from one bracket to the next, for example by hiring an additional employee, the higher EHT rate is incurred not only for the new employee, but also for existing ones. This means that the extra payroll tax incurred by hiring a new employee is higher than it is for existing employees, and is higher for the small firms in the transition set of tax brackets than it is for large firms.

Second, the structure means that if an employer discovers at the end of the year that his or her total remuneration for the year just puts the business into a new bracket, the effective tax rate on the additional remuneration can be unreasonably high. In the most extreme case, $1 of additional pay could lead to additional tax of $484.

The current rate structure has other negative implications for employers and employees. The effective tax rate for a given employee or group of employees is determined by the size of business for which they work, not by any characteristic of the employee. For example, a high-paid employee working for a small employer would be subject to a lower tax rate than a low-paid employee of a large employer. Such distortions cannot be justified on principles of either fairness or efficient operation of labour markets.

If the payroll tax is essentially a tax on labour income, then it is most appropriate to apply a single rate of tax to all such income. We recommend that Ontario eliminate the graduated rate structure for its existing payroll tax and replace it with a uniform rate of tax based on all remuneration. Adoption of this proposal would increase revenue from the Ontario payroll tax by $150 million at current tax rates.

Deductibility of payroll taxes in the corporate income tax

In any consideration of increased reliance on payroll taxes at the provincial level, an important issue is their deductibility for income tax purposes. Current income taxation rules follow accounting practice in treating payroll taxes payable by the employer as a business expense. As a result, an increase in payroll taxes causes a reduction in the income tax base. Accordingly, federal (and provincial) income tax revenues decline as payroll taxation increases, and the impact of new payroll taxes on business is partially offset by reduced income tax payments.

In response to increased use of deductible taxes such as payroll taxes and

capital taxes by some provincial governments, the federal government in 1991 indicated that it intended "to limit the deductibility of provincial payroll taxes and capital taxes from federal corporate income tax" (Canada Department of Finance 1991, 16). Although the actual implementation of limitations on the deduction of payroll and capital taxes has been delayed twice and federal-provincial discussions on the proposal are ongoing, the federal government continues to indicate it will introduce such measures in due course.

These proposals by the federal government would have the effect of limiting the ability of provincial governments to structure their mix of direct taxes to meet provincial priorities. These measures are unfortunate. It is even more regrettable when such steps are taken unilaterally, without recognition of the variety of provincial circumstances. The interdependence of the fiscal systems of the federal and provincial governments is an important feature of the federal system in Canada.

When steps taken by one level of government affect the revenues or expenditures of the other, there is always the potential for conflict. Clearly, there needs to be a more cooperative attitude by all governments. We recommend that Ontario seek the agreement of the federal government to make payroll taxes fully deductible for corporate income tax purposes.

The taxation of small business

In our view, the critical arguments in favour of special tax treatment for small business concern access to financing, the need to encourage high-risk investment, the costs of administration and compliance, and the more general issue of the overall level of taxation on small business.

In our report, we focused on the three provisions that relate specifically to small business: the small business deduction and the related system for personal and corporate tax integration; and the two largest tax expenditures – the flat rate capital tax ($120 million) and the graduated rate schedule in the payroll tax ($150 million), which we addressed previously.

With respect to the paid-up capital tax, we conclude that the current flat rate and graduated rate structure should be retained, largely on the basis that it results in significant savings in administrative costs for government and compliance costs for small businesses.

The small business deduction and integration of personal and corporate income taxation

The small business deduction is the most significant of the special provisions in the Ontario corporate income tax. It results in a reduction in the corporate tax rate from the general rate of 15.5 per cent, or the manufacturing and processing rate of 13.5 per cent, to 9.5 per cent.

When the low small-business rate was introduced federally, the rationale was that small businesses have less access to capital markets than larger firms. The small business deduction means that, after tax, small businesses have more funds available for reinvestment out of each dollar of pre-tax retained earnings.

The small business rate also plays a role in the system of integration of personal and corporate income tax through the special tax treatment of dividend income in the personal income tax. In this system, the taxable amount of dividends is increased to reflect the corporate tax assumed to have been paid on the dividend (the dividend gross-up), and then a credit is granted for the assumed amount of tax (the dividend tax credit).

This mechanism is intended to ensure that income earned through a sole proprietorship and income earned through a small business corporation receive the same tax treatment.

Although the dividend gross-up and tax credit is not exclusively a small business measure, when taken in conjunction with the special low tax rate for eligible small business income, it is a significant benefit for small businesses. Despite the overall value of this benefit, it is not well targeted to the problems of access to capital and compliance costs. The incentive provided through the low tax rate essentially operates as a tax deferral when income is retained in the business and reinvested.

Support targeted directly at these concerns might seem more appropriate. In general, this approach could involve incentives for capital investment (such as investment tax credits), incentives for equity or debt investment, or measures to allow full recognition of losses in the tax system.

However, there are significant problems with these alternatives. Our general conclusion is that the current approach, providing the principal incentive to small business corporations as a reduced tax rate for the first $200,000 of income, should be retained. Several considerations went into this conclusion.

First, the current incentive is available only to those entrepreneurs who have demonstrated the ability to operate a profitable small business, as evidenced by the existence of taxable profits. This provision helps target the benefits of the tax deferral associated with the lower tax rate to investments with a higher likelihood of success. In the case of small businesses, where

Economic Activity

there are many failures, this may be a useful test for eligibility.

Second, all provinces and the federal government provide a lower tax rate on small business income. We have already noted the problems associated with Ontario's attempting to apply tax rates that are out of line with those in other jurisdictions. Although the "mobility of capital" argument may not be as strong in the case of small business as it is for some other investments, we believe it would be contentious and possibly counterproductive for Ontario to deviate significantly from the small business tax structure in place in other provinces.

> *"In a community where there are few large employers and where small business is crucial to job creation, the present complexity of taxes the employer must collect and remit is a disincentive to expansion and the creation of more jobs." ~ Social Planning Council, Thunder Bay hearing*

Third, the current system of small business corporate taxation has been in place for a long time and enjoys a high degree of support not only from the small business sector, but also, apparently, from the broader public. Given the other important changes we are proposing, with implications for the small business sector, it may be appropriate to retain this well-established structural feature intact.

Another reason for retaining the lower small business rate relates to the desirability of treating small business income earned in different ways in a fairly standard fashion. Even if the general provisions for the taxation of dividend and capital gains income are changed, special provisions would still be required to ensure equivalent treatment of business income earned through different organizational forms.

We note, however, that when personal income tax surtaxes are taken into account, the current system does not achieve this result. It contains a bias in favour of income earned through a corporation.

The federal government has adjusted the dividend gross-up and tax credit whenever significant changes in the federal personal and corporate tax rates have occurred. It would be appropriate for the provincial government to take this issue into account as it changes personal rates.

On fairness grounds, the province might also wish to apply a surtax to corporate small business rates in periods when personal surtaxes are in place, as long as this measure is consistent with the objective of the surtax.

The taxation of cooperatives

The cooperative system is a vital component of the business sector in Ontario, particularly in rural areas. Cooperatives are community-based organizations, but, to serve the local level, they also organize at provincial, national, and international levels.

However, despite the fact that more than two million Ontarians report membership in almost 2000 cooperatives, credit unions, and caisses populaires, and the system owns $13 billion in assets, reviews of the tax system often overlook this sector.

To assist in our consideration of cooperative tax issues, the commission established an Advisory Group on Taxation of Cooperatives, composed of volunteer members from a broad spectrum of cooperative enterprises. In the experience of members of the advisory group, cooperatives suffer from "benign neglect" when tax rules are being developed. In some cases, no effort is made to structure the benefits available to other forms of business organization to apply equally to the cooperative

Economic Activity

form of organization. In other cases, rules are introduced or applied in ways that inadvertently affect cooperatives in a negative fashion. We conclude that cooperatives should receive explicit consideration when tax measures are being formulated.

> *"Caisse populaires in Ontario have $2 billion in assets and are a main source of funding for the economic development of francophone communities. Given the economic fragility of this sector, it should not be penalized by tax reform."*
> ~ Association canadienne-française de l'Ontario, Toronto hearing

Our concern about the taxation of cooperatives is whether the tax system works to their disadvantage, relative to other forms of business organization.

We recommend that Ontario consider the ownership and governing structure of cooperatives when developing tax policy, programs, and legislation. Programs should be structured so that:

- the requirements can be met as easily by cooperatives as by other enterprises; and
- the benefits are equally available to cooperatives and other enterprises.

We also recommend an easing of restrictions in the Ontario Investment and Worker Ownership Program that prevent workers from operating businesses acquired under the program as cooperatives. We propose changes to those provisions in the land transfer tax that impose additional tax burdens on cooperative housing developments in which the land and buildings are owned by different cooperative corporations.

Resource taxation

Taxes on natural resources differ from other taxes in that their rationale is not based on the need to raise revenue. In principle, the purpose of the taxes is to recover the value of natural resources held in common for the benefit of society as a whole, but converted from the raw state into marketable products in the private economy.

Resource taxes are intended to establish prices indirectly for products that cannot be priced directly. The goal in designing these taxes is to isolate the underlying value of the resource itself from the profits made by the companies engaged in resource extraction on the assets they employ in the process.

Fairness has a different meaning when applied to resource taxes than to other taxes. A fair resource tax is one that provides the highest return to society on the underlying value of the resource consistent with provincial objectives for employment and economic activity in the industry.

Types of resource taxes

Governments use a variety of special taxes on resources to accomplish this objective. These taxes typically take one of two broad forms: taxes based only on characteristics of the resource product such as severance taxes and royalties; and taxes whose base reflects the economics of particular resource operations and operators such as profits taxes and cash flow taxes.

Royalties and severance taxes

Severance taxes are levied at a flat rate based on the physical amount of the resource product extracted. Royalties are levied as a percentage of the price of the resource.

In neither case does the amount of the tax vary depending on the economics of any particular operation. While this approach may be effective in isolating the underlying value of resources where resource markets are stable and the economics of resource extraction are similar between operators, it is not effective where these conditions do

Economic Activity

not hold. As a result, these types of taxes are most commonly used in forestry taxation and in the oil industry.

Profits taxes

To make resource taxes sensitive to the economics of individual operations, taxes may be based on either the profit or the cash flow generated by each resource operation.

Profits taxes are based on a definition of resource income that is similar to that used in the taxation of corporate income. In fact, these taxes effectively function as special corporate income taxes in the resource sector. While these taxes are responsive to the differences in the economics of resource extraction between operations, they are not effective in isolating the underlying value of the resource product from general corporate profits.

Cash flow taxes

Some observers and analysts have argued for a tax on the cash flow of resource companies as a way to avoid the complexities associated with trying to isolate resource values from normal profits in a profits-based resource tax.

In a cash flow tax, investment costs that are spread out over the life of an asset or project in a profits tax framework would be fully deductible from current income as they are incurred. Capital investment costs as well as operating costs would be immediately deductible. The depreciation or depletion allowances which, in the corporate income tax system, serve to spread these costs out over time would be eliminated. Consequently, there would be no deduction either for depreciation or for interest on money borrowed for capital investment. Any negative cash flow would either generate a tax refund at the rate of tax or be carried forward for deduction against cash flow in the future.

To ensure that a company experiencing a negative cash flow was not placed at a disadvantage compared with a company with a positive cash flow, the negative cash flow carried forward each year for deduction in future periods would be increased by an investment allowance at a predetermined rate of interest to reflect the fact that negative cash flow deducted in future periods is worth less to a company than negative cash flow deducted in the current period.

"The Northern economy is difficult to sustain and depends on the symbiotic relationship between companies, workers and communities. Taxation should recognize and not implement policies which will damage this relationship." ~ Porcupine Developers' Association, Timmins hearing

---

The rate of interest used to adjust negative cash flows carried forward would be set to reflect the cost of forgoing other capital investment opportunities, hence the use of the term "investment allowance." Neither a depreciation allowance nor an interest deduction is necessary because these costs are accounted for in the deduction of capital investment.

A number of mining jurisdictions have introduced cash flow or similar taxes. British Columbia relies on a cash flow base for most of its mining revenue. British Columbia also applies a royalty-based tax to the proceeds of mineral sales net of operating expenditures, but only as a secondary source of revenue. Saskatchewan levies a cash flow tax in the uranium mining industry.

Economic Activity

FIGURE 6

COMPARISON OF ONTARIO MINING
TAX REVENUE UNDER THE CURRENT
SYSTEM AND POSSIBLE CASH FLOW
TAX SCENARIOS, AGGREGATE OF
SAMPLED COMPANIES, 1987–91

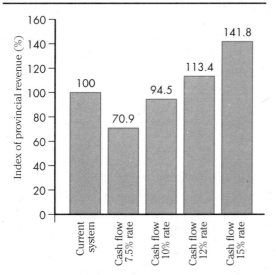

Source: Ontario, Ministry of Finance.

Note: Cash flow scenarios allow immediate write-offs of all capital investments and provide an investment allowance of 12 per cent on any balance. The aggregate sample represents the majority of Ontario's mining tax revenue.

Auctions

Some jurisdictions auction off the right to extract resources in the forestry sector. The idea behind this approach is that the best way to determine the underlying value of a resource in a market economy is to subject the right to exploit the resource to an open bidding process. The difficulty in using auctions as a way to capture the underlying value of a resource is that auctions are effective in doing so only under fairly restrictive market conditions. They do not work effectively where there is substantial risk involved, where there is a limited number of potential bidders, or where one bidder may have a natural advantage over others in exploiting the resource. For this reason, auctions are never used in the mineral sector and are used in the forestry sector only to a limited extent.

A new mining tax system

We believe that a mining tax based on cash flow is the best approach to the taxation of the underlying value of mineral resources in Ontario. This form of tax is particularly well suited to Ontario's mining industry, which is subject to extreme volatility in prices and which consists of mining operations with widely varying production cost structures. Of all the forms of resource tax, a cash flow tax is best able to isolate the underlying value of the mineral resource under these circumstances.

The new mining tax format would bring profound changes to the existing tax. However, elimination of the processing allowance, and current depreciation of assets at differing rates, depending on the type of asset and the age of the mine, should not be viewed as disincentives to mineral investment. In place of these provisions, all operating and capital expenditures would be eligible for immediate deduction. Any portion of the expenditure not deducted immediately would be carried forward for deduction against future receipts, with an investment allowance that approximates a fair rate of return for mineral investment.

The Ontario Mining Tax should also exclude any further deduction for depreciation or interest. Since these features allow full credit for returns on processing assets, there would be no justification for the processing allowance provided for in the current tax system.

Economic
Activity

Cash flow tax rates

Mining taxes and returns on mineral investment in Ontario are comparable to those in other jurisdictions. This suggests that the initial rate of cash flow tax should be set to raise approximately the same revenue as is raised by the current mining tax. A computer model of the Ontario mining industry using data from mining tax returns was developed to examine this option and others. We found that a cash flow tax rate of approximately 12 per cent would generate slightly more than the level of revenues generated by the current 20 per cent tax on mining profits (figure 6).

In establishing rates of tax on cash flow in the mining industry, Ontario should monitor closely world economic conditions in the province's key mineral sectors. Ontario should generate the maximum revenue possible from the underlying value of its resources consistent with the need to maintain the long-term viability of the industry.

Ontario should set the initial rate of the tax on cash flow to generate a long-term revenue yield – after allowing for any tax expenditures – equivalent to the yield of the current tax on profits. A mining tax based on a cash flow format should not provide for exemptions for cash flow below a certain threshold or on any other basis, such as tax holidays for new mines.

The forestry sector

Although cash flow taxation is essentially untried in the forestry sector, we believe there may be potential for the use of cash flow taxes in this sector to recover a greater share of the underlying value of Ontario's forest resource. We recommend that Ontario explore this potential through the Forest Values Project of the Ministry of Natural Resources.

We further believe that, at least as an interim measure, an expanded use of forestry rights auctions, or public bidding for the right to extract the resource, would enhance Ontario's ability to raise revenue based on the underlying value of its forestry resources.

Economic Activity

SALES TAX

Ontario's retail sales tax (RST) is regressive in that a low-income earner pays a greater proportion of income in this tax than a high-income person. It is also a significant source of revenue. In 1991–92 it represented 18 per cent of total revenue, the second largest source of revenue for the provincial government. Although the regressivity of the retail sales tax is of concern to us, given our objective of making the tax system as a whole more progressive, we recognize that it would be impractical to consider eliminating the sales tax from the provincial tax mix.

We focused on three areas in which changes in the design of the tax could improve its performance: the potential for changes in the tax base to improve its relationship to ability to pay; the taxation of business inputs; and administration and compliance costs. We considered each of these issues first on its own merits and then in the context of the relationship between Ontario's sales tax and the federal Goods and Services Tax (GST).

Sales taxes and ability to pay

Regressivity

There are two potential policy responses to the regressivity of sales taxes. One is to change the base of the tax by adding or deleting categories of goods and services from the list of taxable items. The other is to try to offset the regressive impact of the sales tax through transfers to individuals or families, either directly or in the form of tax credits.

We found that, in general, adding or removing items from the list of exemptions does not change the regressivity of the tax. The one major exception is food. Figures 7 and 8 show the proportion of average income spent by households in each income decile group on a number of items that are currently exempt from the retail sales tax. Lower-income families spend a larger proportion of their income on food than they do on goods and services that are currently taxable; higher-income families spend a smaller proportion of their income on food than they do on other goods and services. Thus, adding food to the base would make the tax more regressive. None of the other items would have an appreciable impact on the regressivity of the tax if they were added into the base.

We also examined the use of tax credits to offset the impact of the RST on lower-income households. In 1992 the sales tax portion of the property and sales tax credits was $100 for a single person. With the credits at current levels, however, the sales tax is regressive even after the credit is taken into account.

We concluded that the regressivity of the sales tax cannot be reduced by changing the base of the tax. The extent to which

Sales Tax

FIGURE 7
EXPENDITURES ON FOOD, SERVICES, AND HOME ENERGY AS A SHARE OF
INCOME, ONTARIO, 1991

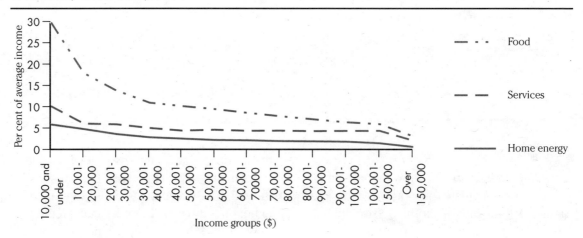

Source: Fair Tax Commission estimates based on Family Expenditure Survey, 1986 (updated to 1991), Statistics
Canada Social Policy Simulation Database and Model (SPSD/M).

regressivity can be offset for low-income families depends on the level of the credits provided in the personal income tax. It is important to note, however, that whatever their level, the credit amounts have nothing to do with the amount of sales tax actually paid by a family. For this reason, we addressed issues related to the tax credit system in the context of our review of provisions for low-income tax relief more generally.

Fair treatment of people in similar circumstances

While changes to the base of the retail sales tax cannot, in general, make the tax less regressive, such changes can affect the impact of the tax on people in similar economic circumstances. Exemptions can result in individuals, whose consumption of goods and services is similar, paying different amounts of sales tax.

For example, one consumer may decide to spend money on dry-cleaning laundry instead of purchasing detergent to wash it at home. The consumer opting for the service of dry-cleaning does not pay RST,

while the taxpayer who purchases detergent pays the tax. Broadening the base for the RST eliminates these discrepancies in the impact of consumer decisions on the fairness of the tax. We believe that the fairness of the retail sales tax would be enhanced if the base of the tax were broadened to include substantially all goods and services, with the exception of food.

Taxation of business inputs

The taxation of materials used in production (known as business inputs) not only increases consumer prices, but also reduces the ability of Ontario's goods and services to compete in export markets. For industries in which prices are set internationally, the taxation of business inputs increases costs for domestic producers.

The portion of the RST on business inputs that falls on investment goods – machinery and equipment, and residential and non-residential construction – also influences the level of investment in the economy. It increases costs to investors, resulting in a lower level of investment in

Sales Tax

plant and equipment. This can have a negative impact on the province's economy.

To estimate the economic impact of removing the RST on different kinds of investment goods, the RST/GST Working Group used simulations, which showed that removing the RST resulted in a 2 to 4 per cent increase in investment in machinery and equipment (above otherwise predicted levels in each year from 1995 to 2000) and a 1 to 3 per cent increase in investment in non-residential construction

A multi-stage sales tax

To remove the tax from business inputs, we recommend a multi-stage sales tax levied on all transactions involving taxable goods and services, with taxes paid on business inputs offset against taxes due from sales.

Under a multi-stage system, all sales are subject to tax. Businesses then claim the credit for any tax paid on purchases, effectively removing the sales tax from all business inputs.

The costs of ensuring compliance are lower for a multi-stage than a single-stage tax. To ensure that purchases on which the tax is credited are actually used for business purposes, only the purchaser needs to be audited, not the supplier.

Reducing compliance and administration costs

In our public consultations, the most consistent complaint raised about sales taxes came from business people who were concerned about the administrative and compliance costs associated with the operation of two independent sales tax systems in Ontario: the federal GST and the Ontario RST.

Most business people who appeared at our public hearings were concerned about the added burden of filing for two separate taxes and what they saw as the unnecessary com-

"Most small businesses went into business to provide a service, but increasingly we are becoming underpaid or unpaid tax collectors." ~ Ottawa hearing

plexity of the current system. Most argued in favour of harmonizing the GST and the RST.

All retailers bear the costs associated with the separate administration and design of the two sales taxes, including the costs associated with dealing with separate administrations, filing separate documents several times a year at different times, and those associated with identifying the tax status of various goods and services. In addition, business must bear the costs associated with audits by two sales tax administrations.

Although no independent estimates are available, the Canadian Federation of Independent Business indicated in its submission to the commission that the additional ongoing cost for small business in 1992 of complying with the GST was $1.2 billion nationally. Assuming Ontario's share would be 40 per cent, the incremental cost associated with this second sales tax is $480 million. The costs associated with separate administration and design could be eliminated, but only through full sales tax coordination with a single administration.

Reducing the Ontario government's administrative costs is another argument for sales tax coordination. However, the savings resulting from full harmonization with joint administration would be relatively small – the total cost of administering the RST in Ontario in 1991 was $40 million. The maximum costs savings would be less than that because of the need for continuing policy review by both levels of government.

A national sales tax

In the current fiscal environment, concerns about administration and compliance costs alone would point towards reform of

Sales Tax

the system. The fact that, structurally, the reformed Ontario sales tax suggested by our analysis is similar to that of the federal Goods and Services Tax strengthens the argument for the development of a single federal/provincial sales tax system.

We are concerned about tax competition among provinces should Ontario harmonize in isolation. This would not reduce compliance costs for firms operating nationally because the greatest savings are realized if harmonization results in identical legislation in each province and a single administration. A "harmonization" that results in different agreements with each of the nine provinces with sales taxes might be worse, from the standpoint of simplicity and economic efficiency, than the current system.

> *"The dual system of GST and provincial sales taxes is one of the most cumbersome and complex regimes in the world."* ~ Retail Tax Force, Toronto hearing

There are a number of other important advantages to a single national sales tax structure. The adoption of a single tax structure would reduce consumer confusion over which goods and services are taxable and which are exempt. Such a change would not prevent Ontario from making rate changes, and the province would also retain the ability to impose selective excise taxes to achieve various policy objectives (such as the Tax for Fuel Conservation).

As auto industry representatives argued at our public hearings, harmonization would place Ontario in a more competitive position because business inputs would no longer be taxed and no tax would be imbedded in the price of goods manufactured in the province.

People living in border communities agreed with harmonizing the two taxes as a way to stem cross-border shopping. At present, the federal government collects

GST at the border on certain items purchased in the United States by Canadians. If the taxes were harmonized, the federal government could also collect the RST, a move that could make cross-border prices less attractive to Canadian consumers.

Issues in harmonization

The main design features of the GST are as follows. Some goods and services are classified as exempt. These goods and services are not themselves taxable, but inputs are taxed without credit. The effect is that these goods and services bear some tax buried in prices, reflecting the tax paid on inputs.

Exemptions include:

- Health care services, financial services, education services, child care services, personal care services, legal aid, resale of homes, and residential rents.

Other goods and services are classified as zero-rated. These goods and services are also exempt from tax. In addition, credits are paid for the tax paid on inputs used in the production of these goods and services. As a result, zero-rated goods bear no tax at all.

Zero-rated goods and services include:

- Basic groceries, prescription drugs, medical services, transportation services, and transit services.

All other goods and services are fully taxable. Most notably, home energy consumption, reading material, children's clothing, and shoes under $30 are exempt in the RST, but taxable in the GST. The general argument in favour of these exemptions is that they offset the regressivity of the sales tax. As we noted above, however, we found that with the exception of food, changes to exemptions have little effect on the regressivity of sales taxes and that they undermine fairness in other ways. We

Sales Tax

FIGURE 8
EXPENDITURES ON READING MATERIAL, CHILDREN'S CLOTHING, AND
PRESCRIPTION DRUGS, ONTARIO, 1991

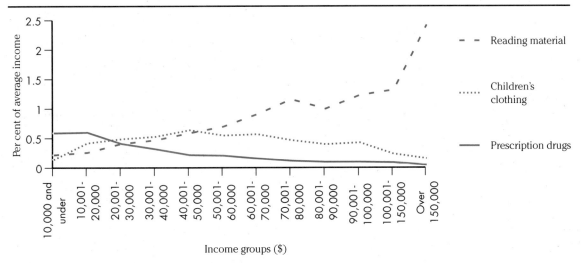

Source: Fair Tax Commission estimates based on Family Expenditure Survey 1986 (updated to 1991), Statistics
Canada Social Policy Simulation Database and Model (SPSD/M).

would therefore be comfortable with a harmonization agreement that results in these
goods becoming taxable.

Taxation of reading material received
particular attention in several of our public
hearings. Reading material is currently taxable in the GST and exempt from the RST.
Strong arguments were presented to us in
support of the exemption for all reading
material, based on the general benefits to
society from literacy and the need to support the publishing industry and promote
Canadian culture.

We decided against an exemption for
two reasons:

- Our research shows that consumption of reading materials increases as
  income increases (figure 8); therefore, exempting reading material
  reduces the fairness of the RST.

- Exempting reading materials from
  sales tax is a badly targeted subsidy
  to Canadian publishers, because 53
  per cent of books and 45 per cent of

periodicals purchased in Canada are
published in a foreign country.

To the extent that support for the
Canadian publishing industry is appropriate, it should be provided directly rather
than through a sales tax exemption for all
reading material, regardless of origin.

We therefore conclude that exemptions in
a national sales tax system should follow the
model in the GST, with two principal exceptions. One recommended departure from
the GST base concerns the tax treatment of
prepared foods. GST applies to prepared
food purchased in restaurants, in cafeterias,
and in home-delivery and take-out establish-
ments, but not to ready-to-serve meals purchased in grocery or convenience stores.
This discriminates against the food services
industry. To equalize treatment, sales tax
should be applied to prepared meals regardless of where they are purchased, as well as
to products that require only limited heat
transfer prior to consumption.

Sales Tax

We also recommend that Ontario seek to extend the sales tax to financial services, which are currently GST-exempt. Provided that administrative problems can be adequately addressed, taxation of financial services could result in a fairer balance between sectors of the economy.

Luxury taxes

There was some support expressed in our hearings for imposing an additional sales tax on "luxury goods."

Based on Canadian and US experience, there are a number of difficulties in trying to use luxury taxes to enhance progressivity of the tax system, particularly in a province like Ontario that is already vulnerable to cross-border shopping. The difficulties include:

- identifying the luxuries themselves;
- tax avoidance and evasion; and
- possible increases in the administrative and compliance costs that must be incurred to collect the tax.

In addition, US experience casts doubt on the effectiveness of luxury taxes in enhancing progressivity in the tax system.

Since the revenue raised by an excise tax imposed only on select "luxury" items is almost certain to be small, the extent to which the tax contributes to the overall progressivity of the tax system is also limited. If the tax were to raise the same percentage of total tax revenue in Ontario as in the United States, it would collect about $5 million annually.

Also, since it is not known who ultimately pays luxury taxes, it is uncertain whether such a tax would actually enhance progressivity or whether the burden of the tax would be shifted to less affluent taxpayers. Indeed, given the opportunities for cross-border shopping in Ontario, it is possible that the ultimate burden of the tax would fall on producers, distributors, and retailers of luxury items in Ontario and their employees.

As a result, we concluded that Ontario should not impose special taxes on luxury items.

Sales Tax

FACING THE ENVIRON-MENTAL COSTS OF OUR BEHAVIOUR

Aside from raising revenue to pay for public services, one of the major uses of the tax system is to provide incentives for individuals and corporations to change their behaviour. These incentives may either be positive (subsidies for activities considered to be desirable) or negative (penalties or fees imposed for activities that are considered undesirable).

The use of taxes for environmental protection is particularly appropriate because many environmental problems arise from actions that are "free" to the individual, but that impose costs on other individuals or groups or on society at large. Properly designed taxes have a potentially important role to play in ensuring that people and institutions face the real costs of actions or decisions that affect the quality of the environment.

The use of tax instruments for environmental protection

Environmental taxes are particularly well suited to situations where the public policy objective is to influence the decisions of large numbers of individual consumers, where regulation is impractical, or where the objective is in part to compensate society generally for the environmental costs imposed on it as a result of individual actions. It is also important, however, that the design of such taxes take into account

"Taxes are not a panacea for dealing with energy problems. People make energy decisions every day – turning on lights, furnaces, air conditioners. We've got to encourage people to conserve and use all policy instruments available to achieve environmental purposes."
~ Canadian Institute for Environmental Law and Policy, Toronto hearing

legitimate concerns about competitive costs and administrative feasibility.

While it would be beyond our mandate to identify all the substances to which environmental taxes might apply, we have decided to focus on four broad areas: carbon taxes; rationalizing the transportation fuel taxes, road-use charges, and the tax on fuel-inefficient vehicles; taxes on ozone-depleting substances; and user fees and taxes for local sewer and water services and solid waste management.

We recommend that Ontario increase its reliance on tax-related economic instruments in its mix of policies for pollution control and resource conservation. Ontario should establish pollution taxes on substances selected from generally recognized pollutants or lists of recognized pollutants, such as the primary and secondary lists of substances for ban or phase-out maintained by the Ontario Ministry of Environment and Energy or the National Pollutant Release Inventory.

Environmental Costs

In establishing its mix of tax, regulation, and other instruments, Ontario should consider the extent to which the tax can be applied directly to the activities generating the pollution and the potential impact of each type of measure on industrial activity.

"Environmental taxes should be a complement to, rather than a substitute for, environmental regulation. (They) should be reduced for companies that demonstrate sound environmental performance … and should be phased in gradually to allow industries time to initiate new … projects." ~ Ontario Forest Industries Association, Toronto hearing

---

A carbon tax

Carbon dioxide emissions are a major factor in global warming, one of the world's major environmental issues.

We believe that the tax system can play a role in influencing the consumption of fossil fuels and therefore the emission of carbon dioxide into the atmosphere. We recommend that Ontario introduce a tax on all fossil fuels consumed in the residential, commercial and industrial, and transportation sectors based on the carbon content of fossil fuel energy inputs.

Our recommendation is tempered, however, by two important factors. First, initiatives in carbon taxation must be seen as small steps towards an international consensus on measures to deal with global environmental problems. For Ontario to step out significantly in front of other jurisdictions would put this province at a competitive disadvantage, and would have relatively little environmental impact. The relationship between Canada and the United States is of particular importance. A general comparison of energy costs between the two countries indicates that costs in Canada may be lower than in the United

States for electricity and natural gas, but higher for coal and industrial oil.

Second, we recognize that the use of fossil fuels is fundamental to the structure and performance of our economy and that changes which influence the prices of these fuels must be introduced in a carefully measured way that takes full account of potential economic implications at every step.

This caution is reflected in our recommendation in three important respects. First, we would suggest only a modest level of tax. A tax of $25 per tonne of carbon content would generate total revenue of about $1 billion. A tax at that level would increase heating bills by approximately $2.85 per month and increase retail gasoline prices by two to three cents per litre. A report prepared for the Fair Tax Commission suggests that, with the exception of a few energy intensive sectors, costs of production would increase by only 0.1 to 0.7 per cent.

Second, we recommend that special policy approaches be taken with respect to the most carbon-intensive industries, which have a limited capacity to respond to a tax in the short term. For example, the only carbon reduction options available to the steel industry involve significant investments in new technologies that have not been proven and could only be made in the long term. We suggest that it might be more appropriate to design special programs for these industries and to exempt them from the tax.

Specifically, for the largest sources of carbon dioxide emissions, we recommend that emission limits be established by regulation or agreement and that a carbon tax apply only if the industries involved fail to meet emission limits.

Third, our discussion suggests that the introduction of a carbon tax should co-incide with reductions in other taxes on business to produce an overall revenue-neutral effect. The intention is not to increase revenue overall. We did not include any estimated revenue from this tax in our tax mix calculations.

Road-use charges and fuel taxes

Ontario levies a variety of taxes and fees that relate in one way or another to road use and the consumption of fuel in the transportation sector. These include the taxes on gasoline and motor vehicle fuels, driver and vehicle licence fees, and the special sales taxes on fuel-inefficient vehicles.

Taxes to support public roads

To determine whether users are paying the full cost of road use, revenues generated by fuel taxes and vehicle registration fees are often compared with road-related expenditures in the province. However, the many functions of current fuel taxes and vehicle registration fees suggest the need for a broader comparison. Together, these charges serve the functions of a provincial sales tax on transportation fuels, an energy tax on transportation fuels, an environmental tax on vehicle emissions, and a fee for road use.

Of the $2.6 billion generated from transportation fuel taxes and vehicle registration fees in 1991–92, approximately $588 million can be viewed as the portion that would be raised by the retail sales tax if it were levied on transportation energy. The remaining $2 billion may be viewed as an excise tax both to reflect the environmental costs associated with transportation energy consumption and to charge drivers for the use of roads and highways.

To reflect the higher environmental costs of fuel use in the transportation sector, the level of tax on transportation fuels should be maintained at a level higher than that

> "... The purpose of taxes is to pay for the governmental infrastructure that enables private and corporate citizens to earn the incomes and create wealth from which the taxes are paid ... Users should be taxed based on their use of infrastructure as it relates to their ability to earn and/or produce."
> ~ Submission, Willowdale

applicable to other fossil fuels in a carbon tax. To the extent that the taxes on transportation fuels function as a user fee for road use, however, there is considerable potential for a rationalization of these taxes, along with vehicle licence fees, to make revenues better reflect the costs associated with road use.

The depreciation of transportation infrastructure varies with frequency of use and vehicle weight. The current system of charges can be viewed as accounting for frequency of use through motor fuel taxes, and for weight through vehicle registration fees. These instruments, however, lack design features that would enable them to reflect such costs more accurately.

We recommend that Ontario establish a new system of vehicle registration based on mileage, vehicle inspection results, and other vehicle characteristics related to road use, such as weight.

Fees raised from this system should replace a portion of the revenue currently raised from transportation fuel taxes. Until this system is implemented, transportation fuel taxes should remain at their current levels.

Commercial vehicle registration fees should be based on distance travelled in Ontario as well as on weight. Ontario should investigate ways of applying this system of charges to out-of-province vehicles so that Ontario companies are not disadvantaged. Truckers based in Ontario and out of the province already keep mileage log books for calculating fuel taxes. These logs

Environmental Costs

might be used to determine kilometres travelled in Ontario and vehicle registration fees owed by all truckers, regardless of origin.

The tax on fuel-inefficient vehicles

Ontario's Tax for Fuel Conservation provides a subsidy or rebate on the purchase of relatively efficient new vehicles and applies a tax on relatively inefficient new vehicles.

One of the gaps in this tax results from the fact that it does not apply to a large proportion of vehicles sold in Ontario. The tax currently applies only to passenger cars and sport utility vehicles. Light trucks and vans are excluded from the tax/credit scheme, although they made up approximately 25 per cent of vehicles sold in the province in 1992.

Even where the tax does apply, its design undermines its potential value as an environmental measure. Current rates of tax as a percentage of the purchase price of the vehicle are probably too low to affect consumer choices to any significant degree. The rate structure contributes further to this ineffectiveness. Because about 90 per cent of passenger cars sold in Ontario currently fall in the fuel-efficiency range that attracts a $75 tax, for practical purposes the tax applies at a flat rate.

Some concern was expressed that a tax on all fuel-inefficient vehicles could apply more often to those produced in Ontario than to imported vehicles, making the Ontario-produced vehicles less price competitive. But much of Ontario's production is exported to the United States and thus is not subject to the tax. In addition, the average vehicle produced in Ontario is relatively more fuel efficient than the average vehicle sold in Ontario, and thus is subject to less tax than imported vehicles.

We recommend that Ontario extend the Tax for Fuel Conservation to light trucks and vans, and then adjust the rates to provide a stronger incentive to purchase fuel-efficient vehicles.

A tax on ozone-depleting substances

We recommend that Ontario introduce an environmental tax on all ozone-depleting substances used in the province, whether new or recycled. The government should ensure that the tax closely complements the province's existing and emerging regulatory framework.

Environmental user charges

The prices charged for water and for sewage and solid waste disposal can influence the amount of solid waste generated and water used. If water is made available free, or at a price that does not vary with the amount consumed, there is no incentive for the individual consumer to conserve water and limit the volume of liquid waste generated.

Similarly, if the cost to the individual of disposing of the solid waste he or she generates is independent of the amount generated, there is no economic incentive to reduce, reuse, or recycle to cut down on the amount of waste for disposal in landfill sites.

One feature of user charges that causes us concern is that, generally speaking, such charges are regressive. While that concern can be addressed in general through changes to the overall mix of taxes, it is important that user fees not curtail access to environmental services by low-income families. User fee systems should include such options as reduced, flat, or constant unit rates up to a minimum level of consumption, subsidized rates for basic service, and exemptions for low-income consumers.

Environmental Costs

Water and sewer user fees

We recommend that user fees be applied for water and sewer services, based on levels of consumption and costs of providing the service. These fees should apply to all sectors that consume these service. Fees for water and sewer services should include a fixed amount to account for the costs of capital replacement, and a variable amount that reflects consumption.

To improve efficiency and to provide incentives for resource conservation, the user fee system should incorporate such features as peak-load pricing, seasonal pricing, and surcharges for hard-to-treat industrial, commercial, and institutional waste.

Solid waste collection and disposal

Residential sector

At present, user fees for waste collection are confined to the industrial, commercial, and institutional sector. Waste generators in this sector generally bear the cost of private or government collection. User charges are generally not applied to residential waste. Until recently, the Municipal Act did not expressly provide local municipalities with authority to impose user fees for residential waste collection.

"In Northumberland, we pay the same amount to dispose of a tonne of garbage as we pay a farmer for a tonne of corn. It's a sad state of affairs."~ Hearings participant, Cobourg

From the perspective of tax fairness, there is no reason why user fees should not be applied for residential waste collection. The user clearly benefits most from solid waste collection and disposal. Nor is there a general public policy reason why the use of this service should be subsidized.

In addition, the reduction of solid waste through user fees would support the Ministry of Environment and Energy's goal of diverting 50 per cent of solid waste from landfill sites by the year 2000. The understandable reluctance of many communities to host a landfill site for Metropolitan Toronto's garbage indicates that reducing the volume of solid waste we produce should be a priority.

We recommend that user fee rates for solid waste in the residential sector reflect all costs associated with its collection and disposal, including the environmental costs generated. Fees should vary with the amount of waste generated. Where possible, fees for residential solid waste should increase with weight.

Industrial, commercial, and institutional sector

The issue of user fees is much more complicated in the industrial, commercial, and institutional (ICI) sector because of the mixture of public and private sector activity in both waste collection and disposal. This means that user fees charged by municipalities for collection and disposal cannot be effective as environmental measures. Increased user fees in the public sector, by themselves, would simply put the private sector operators at a competitive advantage.

The significant role of private operators means that full-cost pricing in the ICI sector can be achieved only through a combination of municipal fees and taxes on private waste collection designed to reflect social costs that would not otherwise be included in the prices charged by private operators.

We recommend that Ontario establish a regulatory and fee framework to ensure that prices charged for solid waste collection and disposal in the industrial, commercial, and institutional sector provide incentives for waste reduction.

Environmental Costs

Taxes on packaging and deposit/refund systems for food and beverage containers

In conjunction with user fees for solid waste, environmental taxes on packaging have considerable promise in effecting changes in consumer behaviour. We recommend a deposit/refund system of environmental charges for food and beverage containers to promote waste reduction objectives first through reuse, and then through recycling.

To be effective, a deposit/refund system should apply to all types of food and beverage containers. The deposit should vary depending on the amount of waste generated by the container when it is dumped in a landfill site. Refunds should vary depending on the use to which the returned container can be put. Containers sent to landfill would not qualify for a refund; containers returned for recycling would qualify for a partial refund, and those returned for reuse would qualify for a full refund of tax paid.

This system should apply to most glass, rigid plastic, and metal food and beverage containers sold in Ontario. This proposed system goes further than those currently in operation in most jurisdictions; in general, deposit/refund systems apply only to beverage containers. If the objective is to limit solid waste generation, however, the system should apply to all containers, regardless of the use to which the container is put. Products bearing a special environmental tax would range from glass soft drink bottles to plastic food containers.

Although studies of the employment impact of deposit/refund systems generally show that these systems are net creators of jobs and economic activity, they offer little comfort to packaging industry employees whose jobs could be affected. New policies to deal with packaging and environmental initiatives more generally must include provisions for employment adjustment.

Environmental
Costs

PROPERTY TAXES IN LOCAL GOVERNMENT FINANCE

Local government finance issues were raised more often in the commission's public consultation process than all other tax issues combined. We received hundreds of letters from individuals and groups concerning property assessment and the financing of education. Most of the community task forces sponsored by the commission found local finance to be the main public issue of tax fairness. Similarly, our public hearings were dominated by discussions with individuals and organizations interested specifically in property tax and the financing of education.

The issues ranged from technical problems with the property assessment system to the broadest questions of public policy. Out of those many individual submissions, some clear messages emerged:

- The system of local government finance is so complex and arcane that most Ontario residents find it incomprehensible.
- Those few who know the system well accept as a given that virtually every component of Ontario's system of local government finance is in a state of crisis or near crisis.
- Most people believe that Ontario is far too dependent on property taxes for the funding of education.

"Property tax is an inappropriate mechanism for funding education. This is a long-term problem that requires a long-term solution ... Right now, it's the students who suffer while we search for a better system." ~Hearings participant, Kingston

- Many Ontarians feel that the current system for funding education discriminates unfairly against students who attend schools with limited access to local sources of funding.
- Business taxpayers consider the business occupancy tax to be unfair; municipal leaders find it difficult to collect, particularly in today's weak economy.
- Municipal leaders question the extent of Ontario's reliance on property taxes for funding social services.
- The system of property assessment and local taxation is extremely confusing and perpetuates a number of obvious inequities.
- Assessment reform, even when introduced in small measures and as a local option, creates its own practical and fairness problems.

Almost without exception, our data and analysis support these opinions. The system of education finance fails to meet its equity objectives for either students or taxpayers.

Local Government

The assessment system is in a shambles. The division of responsibility for taxation and expenditure policy between the provincial government and local governments is hopelessly confused. Our analysis of the specific problems in the system points to more fundamental problems with the fairness of property taxes in their current role in local government finance. We suggest that it would be counterproductive to proceed with reform of any individual component of the local government finance system without first confronting the basic fairness issues in property taxation.

Property taxes and tax fairness

As our discussion of tax fairness suggests, there are two ways to evaluate the fairness of any tax. One looks at the relationship between the tax and the resources available to the taxpayer to pay the tax, applying the ability-to-pay principle of tax fairness. The second looks at the relationship between the tax and the benefits received by the taxpayer from the services funded from the tax, applying the benefit principle of tax fairness.

Our research indicates that the residential property tax is not strongly related to ability to pay, whether ability to pay is measured by income or by wealth, and whether the assessment basis for the tax is the current system, market value, or a system based on the physical characteristics of the property. Our research also indicates that, although many of the services currently funded from property taxes can be fairly funded from local benefit taxes, others cannot be so funded. Specifically, education and social services should be funded from taxes related to ability to pay rather than from benefit taxes.

Residential property taxes and ability to pay

Property taxes and household income

We commissioned one study which used province-wide data to measure the overall relationship between property taxes and household income. It confirmed the general findings of most other studies – that residential property taxes are regressive. Lower-income families pay a higher proportion of their income in property tax than higher-income families.

The regressive pattern was particularly pronounced in the middle and lower income ranges, $50,000 and below. When the provincial property tax credit (administered through the income tax system) is taken into account, households in the $20,000–$30,000 range still pay proportionally more property tax than higher-income households.

Figure 9 shows the overall results of this study. It presents the average percentage of income paid in property taxes by households according to their income.

Households with incomes in the $20,000 – $30,000 range paid out roughly 5.7 per cent of their income in property tax. The property tax credit reduced that average impact by 1.5 per cent – to 4.2 per cent. In the $60,000 – $70,000 range, households paid approximately 3 per cent of their income in property tax. At that household income, the credit had relatively little impact.

The study also found that households in similar financial circumstances pay very different amounts of property tax. In the $40,000 – $50,000 range, half the households pay between 2.5 per cent and 4.5 per cent of their income in property tax. However, one-quarter pay more than 4.5 per cent; one quarter pay less than 2.5 per cent.

FIGURE 9
PROPERTY TAX IMPACT ON HOUSEHOLD INCOMES, ALL ONTARIO RESIDENTS, 1991

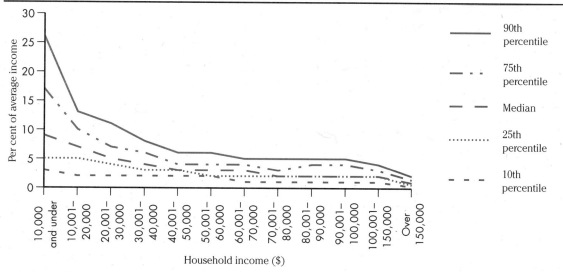

Source: Fair Tax Commission estimate based on Statistics Canada Social Policy Simulation Database and Model (SPSD/M); 1988 data adjusted to 1991 values.

Market value assessment and household income

Another study, which used data on income and the assessed value of property in individual municipalities, showed an extremely weak relationship between household income and the market value assessment of the residential property occupied by the household. In addition, the results showed a similar relationship between any physical characteristics of the property and household income.

Again we found the pattern to be regressive – the property taxes declined as a percentage of household income as income increased. In addition, within income ranges, the assessed value of property and the impact of property taxes on household income varied widely.

The preliminary results of this study showed that, in Pickering, only 3 per cent of the variation in market value assessment could be explained by differences in house-

hold income. In Etobicoke, 7.5 per cent of the variation in assessment could be explained by differences in household income. We also found that no other property characteristic was any better related to household income.

In fact, a poll tax (a flat amount per adult) on income tax filers would have been almost as well related to ability to pay as a market value–based property tax.

The most obvious hypothesis to explain this finding suggests there may be a relationship between life cycle and the value of housing relative to income. It is argued that younger families just getting into the housing market and at the beginning of their earnings cycle occupy property with a higher value relative to their income than older people at a different point in their life and earning cycle.

From this premise, it is argued that these life cycle differences are masking a positive relationship between income and residential property values. Our analysis shows that this is not the case. We found that the relationship between property value and household income was essentially the same, regardless of the age of the head of the household.

These findings are confirmed in another study of the relationship between housing value and family income based on Statistics Canada's 1984 wealth survey. We found that approximately 10 per cent of the variation in property values could be explained by differences in family income. The relationship was stronger than the average for families with children in large urban areas, and weaker than average for other family types and geographical areas. In no case was more than 16 per cent of the variation in property value explained by variations in family income.

The property tax as a wealth tax

It is often argued that, although the property tax may not be closely related to income, it is justified on the basis that it taxes a form of wealth and is therefore related to ability to pay. The argument is that, because other forms of wealth are not taxed, the property tax to some extent offsets a gap in the tax system.

The property tax on owner-occupied property might be seen as a legitimate base for a wealth tax if the value of the residential property occupied by a household serves as a reasonable proxy for the net wealth of the household. Using Statistics Canada's 1984 wealth survey and a report by Ernst &Young based on that survey and other data sources, we looked closely at the relationship between the value of the principal residence and the net wealth of families in Ontario.

> "To most Canadians, a home is not so much an investment in wealth creation, but rather an investment in family, independence and personal dignity."
> ~ Orangeville

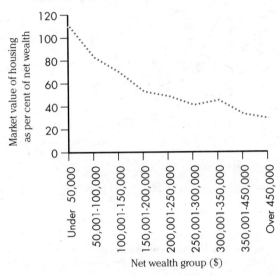

FIGURE 10

MARKET VALUE OF PRINCIPAL RESIDENCE AS PERCENTAGE OF HOUSEHOLD NET WEALTH, 1984

Source: Fair Tax Commission calculation based on Statistics Canada's 1984 wealth survey, microfile for Statistics Canada, *The Distribution of Wealth in Canada, 1984*, Cat. 13-580 (Ottawa, 1986).

Figure 10 shows that as the family's net wealth increases, the value of its principal residence declines as a share of its net wealth. The figure shows that as a wealth tax, the property tax is very regressive.

We also looked at how the relationship between the value of a family's principal residence and its net wealth varies among families in the same wealth group. We found that approximately 25 per cent of the variation in a family's net wealth can be explained by variations in the value of its principal residence.

One group for which this relationship was stronger, however, was families with children living in large urban areas. More than 45 per cent of the variation in net wealth for families in this group was explained by variations in the value of the principal residence.

This suggests that the property tax functions best as a tax on the wealth of families with children. Although this result is not surprising, given that families with children tend to invest heavily in housing, it casts further doubt on the potential role for the property tax as a wealth tax.

Property taxes and benefits received

For many of the services provided by local governments, a property tax based on housing characteristics would appear to be a reasonable proxy for the distribution of the benefits received by property taxpayers. For a second group of services, although property taxes might be a reasonable proxy for benefits, more direct user charges or benefit taxes are available that would better reflect the distribution of benefits. And for a third category of services, there would appear to be no relationship at all between any characteristic of property and the benefits received from the service.

Services such as transportation, planning and development, protection for persons and property, and, to a certain extent, recreation fall into the first category. Although it is obviously not possible to build a direct connection between property taxes and benefit, a general relationship can be demonstrated through an analysis of the particular services and their function within the community.

Sewer and water services and solid waste collection and disposal fall into the second category. As we recommend under the heading of user charges for environmental services, these services should be subject to direct user charges linked directly to the benefit received from using the service.

Education and social services clearly fit into the third category. It would be difficult to argue that there is any relationship between the benefits from education and social services and any characteristic of property.

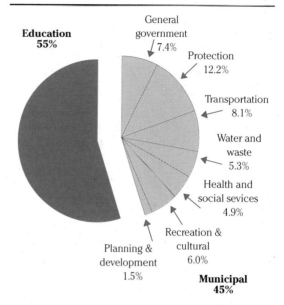

FIGURE 11
USES OF PROPERTY TAX, ONTARIO, 1991

Education 55%

General government 7.4%

Protection 12.2%

Transportation 8.1%

Water and waste 5.3%

Health and social sevices 4.9%

Recreation & cultural 6.0%

Planning & development 1.5%

Municipal 45%

Source: Ontario, Ministry of Municipal Affairs, Municipal Analysis and Retrieval System (MARS).

Education and social services clearly do not fit fairness criteria for benefit taxation outlined earlier. Because benefits from these services accrue to the community at large as well as to the individual, it would be impossible to devise a benefit tax or user charge that fairly reflected the benefit from the service. Even if a tax could be devised that reflected benefit from education and social services, however, it would not be fair to fund these services from such a tax. Both education and social services fail crucial tests for reliance on benefit taxes. In our society, education is considered to be a universal entitlement to which access should not be rationed on the basis of an individual's capacity to pay the cost of providing the service. And both education and social services include in their purposes redistribution of income or equalization of opportunity, either of which would render benefit taxation inappropriate.

Our conclusion, therefore, is that education and social services should not be funded from local property taxes. The local property tax should function as a benefit tax for local services.

A new system for funding education

In the commission's public consultation program, participants singled out a number of aspects of Ontario's system for funding elementary and secondary education as problems:

- Ontario's growing reliance on property taxes as a source of funding for education (figure 12);

- variations in the burden of local taxes required to support education in different parts of the province;

- variations in tax revenue available at the local level in different parts of Ontario and between separate and public school boards; and

- the impact of these variations on the quality of education available to students in different parts of the province.

Why doesn't the current system work?

Under the current funding system, the provincial government defines a level of school board spending per student that it recognizes for provincial support. Grants are allocated by the provincial government to school boards based on a formula that is intended to equalize the tax burden for taxpayers supporting each school board in the province.

There are two problems with this system. First, provincial grant support has been dropping steadily since the mid 1970s. As a result, in most boards the spending recognized by the provincial government bears no relationship to the amount that is actually spent. All the shortfall must be made up from local property taxes.

Second, the grant allocation system attempts to equalize tax burdens for residential and for commercial and industrial property simultaneously. Because assessment systems vary so much from municipality to municipality, tax burdens are not equalized for either class of property.

As a result, the current system of equalized grants does not produce either a fair distribution of spending on pupils or a fair distribution of property tax burdens on taxpayers. Recognized spending in 1993 is, on average, only about 74 per cent of total spending on education at the board level in Ontario. Because local boards are totally dependent on their local assessment base to make up any difference between recognized and actual spending, boards with limited local resources have to choose between imposing higher-than-average taxes to maintain spending levels and reducing program spending to keep taxes in line. Local school boards are thus forced by the funding system to make a trade-off between pupil and taxpayer equity; this trade-off is perceived as unfair by the public.

> *"The local governance of education is a mess ... The property tax system as it is now causes an uneven ability to fund education and services."*
> ~ Hearings participant, Kingston

Reframing the education debate

Our consideration of a new approach to funding education is based on the fairness principles defined by the Property Tax Working Group of the Fair Tax Commission.

Fairness for students

- The overall goal of our system of education, from the perspective of the student, is to enable each student to develop to his or her full potential.

Local Government

FIGURE 12
PERCENTAGE OF ELEMENTARY AND
SECONDARY EDUCATION COSTS
FUNDED FROM PROPERTY TAXES,
ONTARIO, 1970–92

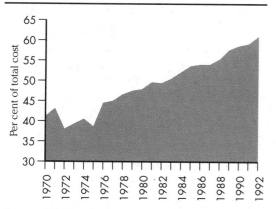

Source: Fair Tax Commission calculation based on
Ontario, Ministry of Education administrative data.

Equality of opportunity, access, and quality of service are important targets in our system of education as proxies for this overall goal.

- The ability of the education system to deliver provincially mandated services to students in Ontario should not depend on local financial resources.

- Educational equity may require that per student spending be different across Ontario. Any funding formula must be sensitive to local needs and circumstances and must allow local boards to deliver programs that respond to the different circumstances of individual students.

Fairness for taxpayers

- In principle and to the extent that it is feasible, education should be funded from revenue sources based on ability to pay.

- The decision to provide education through local school boards should not result in significantly different tax burdens being imposed on taxpayers in different jurisdictions for provincially mandated standards of service.

Three further principles arise from these fairness propositions:

- The provision of education that is universally accessible should be the responsibility of democratically elected government as a cornerstone of a liberal democratic society, as a vehicle for bringing together diverse cultural values and identities, and as a key to sustainable economic development in the future.

- Since all Ontarians are equally entitled to education that supports lifelong learning, the ability of education systems to provide that education should not vary according to the amount of money that can be raised locally.

- The distribution of centrally allocated funds for publicly supported education should vary only according to geographic or demographic variations in the costs of meeting needs fairly and equitably.

The debate over the funding of education has traditionally begun with the assumption that the property tax must provide the core funding. This assumption distorts discussions about both fairness for taxpayers and fairness for students. Discussions about fairness for taxpayers traditionally focus on finding ways to alleviate inequities created by the reliance on property taxes. The debate is dominated by such issues as taxation on farmland, cottage properties, and the homes of senior citizens; or by how much relief the province should provide to individual property taxpayers and to school boards in the form of grants to school boards to reduce the property tax portion of education revenues. Discussions about fairness for students (expressed as per pupil funds available) traditionally focus on which institutions have access to which property tax revenues. The result is that "poor" school boards square off against "rich" school boards, and public boards of education are pitted against Roman Catholic separate school boards over access to commercial and industrial property taxes.

Lost in this debate is any sense of the principles that determine how much and by what means taxpayers should pay for a publicly supported education system. Equally lost is the sense of what education taxes are supposed to be funding in the way of guarantees to the students themselves and to the broader society of which they are a part.

The debate about how schools are actually run never gets started because property tax funding locks in the assumption that school governance has to be established as a parallel system to municipal governance.

Our analysis takes the debate over education taxation and funding back to the basics of fairness. On the one hand, this means fairness for taxpayers whose burden should be more closely related to the ability to pay. On the other hand it means fairness for all students whose learning should not be compromised by accidents of geography, socio-economic status, or ethnocultural origin.

Our recommendations propose a framework designed to meet fairness objectives for taxpayers and students throughout the system and to provide local decision makers with the fiscal capacity to undertake initiatives that respond to local needs and conditions.

Fairness for students

Equity for students does not mean equal funding for every student, and equity for students is not possible without adequate funding.

We recommend that the provincial government assume responsibility for the funding of education, allocating funds to school boards based on per student cost, student needs, and community characteristics.

"A child in an assessment poor area is no less deserving of the funds available for education than a child who has the good fortune to live in an assessment rich area."
~ Hearings participant, Windsor

Determining what constitutes an adequate level of funding for the education of students in Ontario and how that funding should be allocated among schools is an extremely complex task that transcends our tax fairness mandate. The nature of the debate over education finance reform that took place in our public consultation program and in the Property Tax Working Group makes clear, however, that our proposed tax fairness reforms will not be accepted unless they are accompanied by reforms in funding and allocation.

Concerns about overall adequacy in funding need not necessarily be met with increased funding for the educational system as a whole. We repeatedly heard concerns about the proportion of the education budget that is spent outside the classroom.

In allocating funding for education, we have identified a number of factors we believe should be taken into account in creating a formula that meets the expectations for flexibility and responsiveness to local needs. Such a formula must ensure that a foundation level of education is fully funded throughout the province from revenues collected and disbursed centrally. It must recognize the relationship between demographic characteristics of student communities such as socio-economic status, mother tongue, and household literacy, and the level of service (and therefore spending) needed to ensure equity for students.

Fairness for taxpayers

We recommend local residential property taxes be replaced as a source of core funding for education in Ontario with funds raised from provincial general revenues. We also recommend that Ontario eliminate the local education levy on commercial and industrial property and raise these funds from provincial general revenues through the introduction of a provincial tax on commercial and industrial property. The revenue sources required at the provincial level to replace the local residential property tax, and the design of the proposed provincial tax on commercial and industrial property, are addressed in the context of our discussion of the provincial tax mix.

We considered as an option the approach taken in some other jurisdictions of maintaining local funding for school buildings and other physical facilities, with provincial funding for all other educational requirements. This would have left about 10 per cent of education costs to be funded at the local level. We concluded, however, that it would be arbitrary to attempt to distinguish for funding purposes between the classroom itself and what goes on in the classroom.

Local discretionary spending

Educational equity requires unequal funding in ways consistent with different cost factors and needs of different student populations. A successful funding model must also be dynamic. It must be adjusted constantly to respond to changing demographic trends and educational requirements. And it must be consistent with a locally responsive system of governance.

In determining an appropriate design for the financing of local educational expenditures beyond those approved and supported by the provincial government, we considered four critical questions:

- What should the funding base be for locally supported educational spending?
- How should access to that funding base be limited?
- How should that funding base be allocated between the public and the separate systems?
- How should the local political decisions be made with respect to access to that funding base?

To be consistent with our reasoning with respect to appropriate revenue sources for provincially supported education spending, we should recommend a local income tax for discretionary local education spending. However, we are not prepared to recommend the establishment of local income taxes in Ontario. As a result, the only general tax base available for the funding of discretionary local spending is the local property tax base.

The capacity of school boards to raise funds from the local residential property tax base to supplement provincial funding for education should, however, be strictly limited. The levy should be limited to the residential property tax only. The total levy for any school board should be limited to a fixed percentage, not greater than 10 per cent, of the total amount of provincial funding provided to the local school board.

Access to the property tax base must be tightly restricted to preserve its role as a formula funding safety valve, to ensure that pressure is kept up on provincial governments to maintain a realistic level of formula funding for education, and to limit the potential for revenue-driven inequities to emerge for students in different parts of the system.

Local Government

Assessment and property tax reform

A patchwork quilt of inconsistencies

The province took over the property assessment function from municipalities nearly 25 years ago, in an attempt to develop a single system of assessment for all property in Ontario based on market value. Today, the system is still in disarray.

The assessment system is a patchwork quilt of inconsistent approaches that frustrates attempts by governments to achieve fairness in local government finance and by taxpayers to understand how their property tax bills work. Property is assessed at a percentage of market value that varies from municipality to municipality. Within each municipality, this percentage varies for different property classes.

> *"Fairness means equal taxes for equal dwellings, regardless of the yardstick used to measure them ... The rules applied to property assessment are irrational and incomprehensible. This makes them unfair."~ Hearings participant, Thunder Bay*

As a result, it is difficult to compare tax burdens in different municipalities. Similar properties may be assessed and taxed very differently in different parts of the province.

Assessment differences also lie at the root of issues in local government finance that initially appear unrelated to assessment. For example, residential property taxes for education are extremely high in Peel and York regions compared with residential taxes for education in Metropolitan Toronto. Although at first glance it would appear that the difference can be explained by differences in the size of the commercial and industrial assessment base between Metropolitan Toronto and the surrounding area, it turns out that differences in the basis used for assessment in these areas contribute significantly to the problem.

If the assessed values of commercial and residential property are adjusted to reflect market values in a common base year in Peel and York, commercial property is taxed at about the same rate as single family residential property. On the same adjusted basis in Metropolitan Toronto, commercial and industrial property is taxed at roughly twice the rate of residential property. Depending on one's perspective, either commercial and industrial taxpayers in Metropolitan Toronto are subsidizing single family residential taxpayers, or single family residential taxpayers in Peel and York are subsidizing commercial and industrial taxpayers. In fact, compared with the provincial average relationship between single family residential and commercial properties, each of these perspectives is about half right.

The system preserves as many different local taxation policies as there are municipalities. These different policies exist behind the facade of a legally mandated relationship between tax rates on different classes of property. The Education Act, the Municipal Act, and the Ontario Municipal Unconditional Grants Act require that the rate of tax on residential property be 85 per cent of the rate of tax on non-residential property. Implicit in this requirement is an expectation that all residential property will be taxed at the same rate and that all commercial and industrial property will also be taxed at the same rate.

In practice, none of the tax rate relationships among different classes of property comes close to matching the standards set in legislation. Relationships between effective tax rates on different classes of property are diverse across municipalities for both residential and non-residential properties.

We analysed the impact of property taxes across the four principal property classes (residential with fewer than seven units, residential with seven or more units, commercial, and industrial) and found that, in general, rental residential property is the most heavily taxed. Industrial property is the next most heavily taxed, followed by commercial property. Owner-occupied single family residential property is taxed at the lowest effective rate.

Understanding the property tax system

During our public hearings, we heard repeatedly from frustrated, angry, and dissatisfied taxpayers who received assessment notices they didn't understand; who were given explanations of figures that didn't make any sense; and who participated in an appeal process in which the points at issue were never clear, the real issues never discussed, and the process itself, they felt, was biased against them.

From the taxpayer's perspective, the local government finance system is nothing short of impenetrable. The role of assessment in relation to tax is mysterious. In most areas, three distinct levels of government – lower-tier (local) municipal, upper-tier (regional, district, county, and metropolitan areas) municipal, and school boards – determine portions of the tax rate. Local politicians regularly blame the provincial government for tax increases. The provincial government regularly accuses local politicians of fiscal irresponsibility.

Options for assessment reform

In our framework for property tax fairness, the property tax is intended to serve as a proxy for benefits from municipal services that provide benefits to the local community. In keeping with this role, the objective in

designing an assessment system should be to find a basis for assessment in which property assessments serve as a reasonable proxy for the distribution of benefits from local services. We looked at four types of systems: market value, two-tier, rental value, and unit assessment.

Market value

The introduction of region-wide market value assessment in Ottawa, and proposals to introduce it in dynamic and diverse property markets such as Toronto, Halton, and Hamilton, have underlined both conceptual and practical problems with the market value model for assessment reform.

Although market value sounds simple as a concept, it is difficult to estimate on a consistent basis. Different methods for estimating it produce different results because they are measuring different things.

The market value of a property consists of two components: the value of the property in its current use; and the value attributable to potential future uses. The varying roles of these components in determining the market value of a property contribute significantly to the practical and conceptual problems associated with the implementation of market value as an assessment base.

> "MVA is not a fair tax when a year of peak real estate values is chosen as the year for reassessment ... For market value assessment to be fair to all, it must accurately reflect current market value."
> ~ Burlington

As a practical matter, the three primary bases used by assessors to measure market value – arm's-length sales, rental income, and replacement value – differ in the extent to which they measure the components of value. Arm's-length sale prices measure the components of value together because they represent what a buyer would pay for full enjoyment of the rights of ownership.

Local Government

Rental income measures only the value of a property in its current use. Replacement value reflects value in current use, but may be higher or lower than that value – for commercial and industrial assessments, this could depend on conditions in the industry under consideration.

The method used for assessment depends in part on the type of property involved and on the purpose for which the assessment is being undertaken. The particular method used for estimating market value influences the final assessment. For example, in the residential sector and the commercial sector, both the arm's-length sales method and the rental income method are used for valuing different types of properties. Because arm's-length sales data reflect components of value not reflected in rental income, properties valued using the former method will tend to be overvalued relative to properties valued using the latter method.

In the commercial sector, large commercial properties and shopping centres are valued using the rental income method. Smaller commercial properties in "strip retail" areas (stand-alone stores with individual street frontages) are valued using arm's-length sales as the assessment method. In the residential sector, large multiple-unit rental buildings are assessed using the discounted rental income method; single family residences and small rental properties are assessed using arm's-length sales data. In the commercial sector, the effect of these assessment inconsistencies has been quite visible in rapidly growing large urban areas where market value assessment reform has been considered. In the residential sector, the effect has not been apparent because most areas with significant multiple-unit residential sectors have been reassessed, keeping multiple-unit properties as a separate class from single family and small multiple residential properties.

In the current system, assessors determine the method to be used in assessment. Because the results depend in part on the choice of assessment method, various factors are developed to adjust the various results to a common base. For example, rental income is adjusted using a pre-determined rate of interest to discount the value of future rental income to a current lump sum value. The use of these factors does not, however, overcome the problem that the underlying values are determined using different approaches.

The use of a measure of value that includes values attributable to potential future uses or changes in value contributes to volatility in measured market values. Because values attributable to future capital gains or potential uses are essentially speculative, they tend to vary dramatically with the business cycle and with the health of the local economy.

Two-tier assessment

A number of participants in our public hearings and in the Property Tax Working Group advocated a change from market value assessment to two-tier assessment. Two-tier assessment is a variant of market value assessment in which land and improvements are assigned market values separately and are taxed at different rates. Although it is obviously possible to tax either improvements or land at a higher rate, the arguments for two-tier assessment imply that land would be taxed more heavily than improvements.

The principal argument in favour of two-tier assessment is a planning argument. Specifically, it is argued that two-tier assessment will create incentives for intensification of land use and more rapid economic development because two-tier assessment would permit municipalities to impose taxes at higher rates on land than on buildings.

The major problem with two-tier assessment is that Ontario's urban planning and economic development objectives are not one-dimensional. In some areas, the public policy goal is to encourage the development of land to its maximum intensity. For example, one goal may be to encourage re-development of vacant land in downtown areas or along transportation corridors. In other areas – preservation of agricultural land or heritage buildings, for example – the objective of planning policy is explicitly to discourage land from being developed to its highest and best use. In some situations, the goal may be to protect older industrial areas from encroachment by residential or commercial developments, or to promote neighbourhood stability by discouraging land assembly and redevelopment in residential areas. As a planning tool, two-tier assessment is far too blunt an instrument to be considered as a reasonable substitute for, or even a complement to, coherent and sophisticated planning and development policies.

More important, two-tier assessment and taxation would exaggerate the one characteristic of market value assessment that is most undesirable from a benefit tax perspective: the value measured includes values attributable to future uses of the property and future potential capital gains. Because the locational attributes that give rise both to potential future uses and to increases in value in excess of inflation attach to land rather than to buildings, two-tier assessment and taxation would increase the weight given to these non-use related values.

Rental value

The most direct way to measure the value of a property in its current use is to measure its value as a rental property. Since a tenant is not paying either for the right to earn a future capital gain or for the right to change the use of the property in future to a higher-value use, rent is a direct measure of current use value. For properties that are normally offered for rent, measurement of rental value is relatively straightforward. For residential and non-residential properties that are not on the rental market, rental values must be estimated from market data.

It is apparent from the discussion above that rental value would be a better proxy for benefits from services delivered than market value.

Unit assessment

Assessment systems based on physical measurement, or unit assessment systems, clearly offer advantages of simplicity, transparency, and administrative ease. Physical measurement systems avoid the problem of valuation in the absence of a transaction because the assessment of the property is based on an objective determination that can be reproduced by the taxpayer without expert assistance. We have concluded that while an assessment system based on physical measurement would be extremely economical to administer, the insensitivity of such a system to differences in quality and location of property would result in assessments that do not adequately reflect benefit from local services.

Unit value assessment

One approach, which would be consistent with actual practice in the current system, would be to establish rental values per square foot for various categories of property and then calculate individual assessments based on category and area. This approach would, in concept at least, be similar to mass assessment techniques currently used by provincial assessors in measuring market values. The issues to be resolved in assessing a property would include determination of the property category, definition of areas for which different value factors might apply,

Local Government

physical measurement of the property, and measurement of value per square foot by property category and area. Values, categories, and areas would be determined within a municipality on the basis of available rental data. Appeals related to physical measurement or category allocation would be dealt with on an individual basis. Appeals related to the determination of rental value factors would be dealt with through a broader public hearing process.

A new residential assessment system

Residential assessment should not be based on the value of property in exchange or market value.

We believe assessment of individual properties for local taxation purposes should be based on the following factors:

- size of building,
- dimensions of lot, and
- type of building.

Weighting factors used in combining the elements of size of building and dimensions of lot for each type of building should be designed to ensure that the resulting assessments reflect variations in the value of properties in their current use.

Weighting factors would be permitted to vary based on location, subject to the following restrictions:

- Assessment areas could not be smaller than geographically connected areas that carry the same zoning designation for planning purposes.
- Different weighting factors based on location would be established to achieve assessments that reflect value in current use.

For the assessment of residential properties, we were attracted to unit assessment systems for their administrative simplicity and clarity. Assessment based on some combination of lot, building area, and building type would be easily reproduced by the owner of a property, would require little judgment by the assessor, and would simplify enormously the appeal process.

As attractive as unit assessment is for its simplicity, a number of considerations led us to recommend a modification of the unit concept in order to introduce elements related to the value of property in its current use, or rental value.

First, assessment based on a combination of building area and lot area would require the adoption of weighting factors to be used in adding the various elements of the assessment together. The introduction of building type as another variable in a unit assessment system would require the adoption of different weighting factors to be used for each type of building. We believe these weighting factors should not be determined arbitrarily, but should reflect some underlying principle that would establish the relationship between the assessments of different types of properties.

Second, we conclude that residential properties in more advantageous locations, as reflected in the general rental values in those locations, receive a greater benefit from certain public services than do residential properties in less advantageous locations. For example, residential properties located close to rapid transit facilities receive greater benefit from the public transit system than residential properties located on bus routes on the fringe of urban areas.

Third, studies of unit assessment in the City of Toronto in 1986 indicate that the introduction of a pure, unweighted unit assessment system in the single family and duplex residential category would have generated substantial shifts in assessment away from the wealthiest areas of the city and towards the poorest areas. We believe that local govern-

Local Government

ments would find it extremely difficult to justify such shifts on a benefits principle.

We believe that a system of unit assessment based on building area, lot area, type of building, and location, modified by requiring that the resulting assessments reflect variations in value in current use of residential property, would retain much of the simplicity and transparency of unit assessment from the perspective of the individual property tax payer. At the same time, it would recognize the importance of locational values as a reflection of benefits from local services.

In addition to requiring that the resulting weighted assessments reflect values in current use or rental value of residential properties, we believe it is important to impose some restriction on the definition of assessment areas or locations.

Although there is no inherent reason why any one restriction would be preferable to any other, there is some value in selecting as the basis for such a restriction geographical areas that are already recognized for some other purpose. One potential basis that offers some advantages would be to limit assessment areas to geographically connected areas that have a common zoning category.

We also believe there is no justification for the existence of a distinction in the tax rates on the basis of the type of tenure enjoyed by the occupant of the dwelling unit under consideration. We recommend a one-class system – all residential property should be assessed on the same basis without reference to whether the property is occupied by an owner or a tenant.

Impact on tenants

Tenants are overtaxed compared with single family homeowners. In most municipalities, multiple-unit residential properties are assessed at between two and three times the rate of single family homes.

> "All tenants should be treated equally. The concept that tenants are a separate class of people is the root of this problem. They pay so much tax, it accounts for between three and four months' rent a year."
> ~ Landlord-Tenants' Association, Toronto hearing

Because a common tax rate is applied to the assessed values of all residential properties, this results in tenants paying taxes at a higher effective rate than homeowners.

Our recommendations on the taxation of residential property would result in substantial reductions in property taxes on rental residential property for two reasons. First, rental residential property would benefit along with other residential property from the replacement of property taxes as a source of core funding for education. Second, assessment reform within the residential sector at the local level would generally result in significant tax reductions for rental property relative to owner-occupied residential property. These changes are intended to reduce the level of property taxation borne by residents, not to improve the profit picture of residential landlords.

As a result, it is essential that mechanisms be put in place to ensure that reductions in property taxes resulting from these changes are passed on to tenants. Changes in local government finance with respect to rental residential property should not be implemented until a means of ensuring that tenants receive the benefit of those changes is in place.

We recommend that residential tenants be made aware of the assessment and corresponding local benefits taxes that are applicable to the property they occupy and are reflected in their rents. For information purposes, municipalities should be required to send property tax notices to all tenants, itemizing all taxes applicable to their units.

Local Government

Commercial and industrial assessment

We recommend that all non-residential property be assessed on the basis of the rental value of the property – that is, the price that would be paid for property of that class and type for the right to employ the property in its current use. This concept is much easier to apply in the commercial and industrial sector than in the residential sector because well-established rental markets exist for most types of commercial and industrial property.

In our framework, the base for the commercial and industrial property tax as a local benefits tax should reflect the value of the property in its current use. As is the case with the residential property tax, since the goal in designing a base for a commercial and industrial benefits tax is to reflect benefits from local services, it makes no sense to include in the base values attributable to potential future gains or potential future uses. A store located on land zoned for high-rise development does not receive greater benefit from local public services than a similar store located on land zoned for a two-storey walk-up building. Therefore, it would not be appropriate to tax the store based on its value as a site for a high-rise building.

Unique properties

Railway and utility rights of way, single purpose industrial properties, cemeteries, and churches are examples of properties for which conventional assessments do not work. We believe non-residential properties whose value in current use is difficult to determine should be subject to statutory assessment rates.

Rights of way are unserviced, mostly inaccessible strips of land that cannot be used for anything other than their present use. They have no development potential and, when abandoned, have been demonstrated to have only marginal value on the market. They should be assessed at provincial standard unit rates that are updated on a regular basis as assessed values generally are updated.

The assessment of churches and cemeteries is not a problem under the current system. Although churches and cemeteries are theoretically assessed at market value like all other properties, they are exempt from tax. As a result, their assessment has no impact on their tax liability. In our recommendations concerning exemptions from local property taxes, however, we recommend that these properties no longer be exempt. Rather than attempt to determine a value in current use of these properties, they should be assessed at a standard unit rate.

Assessment of vacant land

Where a property is in use or is available for use for an economic purpose, identifying the use of the property is relatively straightforward. In many cases, however, there is no current use for the property, or the property is underutilized. Properties such as a surface parking lot zoned for other purposes are simply being held as investments based on future use potential.

While such properties would have little or no value in current use, their owners clearly benefit from local public services. It would not be fair, therefore, to exempt vacant land from taxation, or to assess underutilized properties at a value reflecting only their current use. The difficulty is how to assign an assessed value fairly to such properties.

The benefit principle provides no useful guidance. Assessment based on the previous use of the property would be somewhat artificial. Assessment based on the highest and best use permitted by zoning would base assessment on a use which may never be realized.

Local Government

In our view, the best guide to assessing the probable future use of a property would be to look at similar properties in the vicinity whose use has recently changed. Such a basis for assignment of use also has the advantage of providing the appropriate incentive to landowners from a planning perspective. The incentive built into the system would be to maintain property in use until it is ready to be redeveloped. Therefore, we recommend that vacant land be assessed based on the preponderant use of property in the area.

Assessment of recreational trailers

Issues related to the assessment and taxation of mobile recreational trailers and trailer parks played a prominent role in our public hearings.

Trailer park operators pointed out that many trailers are located on a given site for only one season, making it difficult for owners to collect property taxes from seasonal occupants of trailer parks. Differences in values of trailers would make adding tax to the ground rent in the trailer park an unrealistic solution. Park operators urged us to support the recommendations of an interministerial committee of the provincial government, an approach that called for the introduction of an annual permit fee for all trailers located in campgrounds for more than 90 days and occupied by persons who have a principal residence elsewhere. Trailers occupied by persons who do not have a principal residence elsewhere would be assessed and taxed.

We accept that assessment of recreational vehicles and mobile trailers would be impractical and would impose an onerous administrative burden on trailer park operators.

We recommend that a flat amount be used as the basis for taxation rather than an assessed value. At the same time, however, we do not believe that the position taken by trailer park operators adequately addresses the concern expressed by municipalities and cottagers that residents of trailer parks consume municipal services equivalent to those consumed by cottage residents and should be required to pay taxes on a comparable basis.

The fee should be set by the provincial government at a level that reasonably reflects a pro-rated portion of the property taxes that would typically be paid on the unit if it were permanently attached to the land and taxed as a residential property.

Fees would be collected by campground or trailer park operators and remitted to the local municipality or, in an unorganized territory, the local roads board. Trailers for which mobility is impaired by their installation on a site would be assessed and taxed as residential property.

Benefit taxation and local finance

In addition to our core recommendations for reform of education finance and the assessment system in the province, we make a number of other recommendations that flow directly from the benefit tax framework we adopted for a fair local property tax system.

Local tax rates

Consistent with our treatment of the residential and non-residential property taxes as separate taxes, we recommend that Ontario abandon the requirement that the residential tax rate be 85 per cent of the non-residential tax rate.

Instead, we recommend that there be no restrictions on residential tax rates and that non-residential tax rates be subject to a minimum rate established by the provincial government to prevent municipalities

Local Government

from using non-residential tax rates as a basis for competition for development with other Ontario municipalities.

Taxation of seasonal and recreational properties

At many of our hearings, cottagers maintained they should not have to pay some of the local taxes they currently pay because they cannot fully benefit from locally provided services. In particular, cottage and recreational property owners argue they should not have to pay local taxes to support municipal services not available to them as seasonal residents. We also heard arguments that cottagers should not be required to pay local education taxes.

Our recommendations address these concerns to a certain extent. The removal of core funding for education from the residential property tax will reduce these taxes on cottage and recreational property as it does for all other residential property. In addition, our recommendations for increased reliance on user fees for sewer, water, and solid waste collection and disposal services would link service costs directly to use.

However, we cannot accept the premise on which the broader argument concerning municipal taxes and services is based. We do not see the property tax as a benefits tax tied to the use of particular local services and cannot support the idea that property taxes should be rebated to taxpayers if they do not or cannot use a particular service.

Certain taxpayers should not be exempted from paying for particular elements of the package of local services funded from property taxes on the grounds that they derive less benefit from those services than other taxpayers.

With respect to education funding, as long as property taxes remain a source of funding for education in Ontario, we can

> *"Property tax in an inappropriate mechanism for funding education. It's a long-term problem that requires a long-term solution. Every citizen and every taxpayer should contribute to the education of our children. But not twice."* ~ Hearings participant, London

see no justification for exempting cottages and recreational property from those taxes. In particular, we do not believe that ownership of a second residence should cause the owner to qualify for an exemption from local taxation on one of them.

As far as our recommended system is concerned, the only local education tax remaining would be a limited local discretionary levy. We believe that all local levies on residential property should apply in full to all properties taxed as residential property, whether they are used as principal residences or for recreational purposes.

The taxation of farming property, woodlots, and wetlands

We believe the current practice of assessing the farm residence and one acre of land as residential property should continue.

However, we see no reason why farming property other than the residence and one acre should continue to be taxed as residential property. Farming should be considered for property tax purposes to be a commercial/industrial activity. It should be assessed and taxed on the basis of its value in current use or rental value, based on available provincial data on soil quality and productivity, and taxed locally as commercial and industrial property.

Although we heard extensive submissions from farmers arguing for an exemption from municipal taxes as well as from education taxes, we cannot accept the argument that farming property should be exempt from property taxes levied for local services.

With respect to property taxes for education, we recommend a different approach consistent with our general framework for education finance. As residential property, the farm residence would be subject to any local discretionary education levy on residential property. As non-residential property, the farm other than the residence would not be subject to a local levy for education. As commercial property, however, it would normally be subject to a property tax levied by the provincial government.

However, for reasons outlined in our discussion of provincial taxation of commercial and industrial property, we concluded that farming property should be exempt from that tax.

"Forest land is valued at the value which the land would have, if there were an alternative use. Forests close to urban areas could be used for urban development and with current assessment principles, could result in taxes which would force the owner to 'liquidate' the forest."
~ Ontario Forestry Association, Mississauga hearing

Similar tax treatment should be provided for managed forests and wetlands. They should be assessed based on their current use and subjected to local taxation on that assessment. These types of properties should be exempt from the provincial commercial and industrial property tax.

Provincial grants policy

As a result of our analysis of the relationship between property taxes and the services currently funded from property taxes, we concluded that services which should not be funded from benefit taxes, such as education, social assistance, and assistance to children, should be funded by the provincial government from provincial general revenue.

A similar logic led to the conclusion that services such as sewer, water, and solid waste collection and disposal should be funded from direct user charges. The local property tax would then play the role of a benefit tax for local services of general benefit to the community.

The same logic suggests that provincial grants should be used to support local services only in special circumstances. We therefore recommend a review of provincial support programs for local services, with a view to restricting provincial support to services that generate benefits outside the local area and to situations in which local conditions make basic services unaffordable.

We recommend that payments to support basic services be equalized to a standard tax rate for non-residential property and to a standard impact on the household income of residents of the municipality for residential property.

We anticipate that application of these criteria could result in a significant reduction in provincial grants for strictly local services. These recommendations are also consistent with recommendations from a number of reviews in recent years for disentanglement of the provincial/local financial and program relationship.

Funding regional, district, metropolitan, and county governments

In a benefits framework, the allocation of costs of upper-tier government should be based on residential and non-residential assessment. With a revised assessment system as recommended by the commission, this would be relatively straightforward.

The approach we recommend would base shares of upper-tier costs on actual tax policies in the previous year. Each municipality's share would be based on what its share of total taxes in the upper-tier area would have been if it had taxed residential and non-residential property at the average rates for these types of property. This share, combined with the budget for the upper-tier area, would generate a local share of upper-tier costs for the lower-tier area.

Each lower-tier municipality would be free to determine the allocation of its share of upper-tier costs between residential and non-residential taxpayers in its local area, subject to any applicable provincial restrictions on tax rates.

Infrastructure funding

As a direct implication of our approach to education funding, we recommend that the use of lot levies for education funding be abolished.

We also recommend that lot levies for municipal services be restricted so that they cannot be used to fund capital expenditures that arise simply because the population or total employment of the community has increased. They should apply only to the extent that property taxes on new developments cannot be expected to generate sufficient revenue to pay for the required infrastructure.

Other local government finance issues

In addition to the issues that arise directly from our framework for property tax fairness, we make recommendations on two other major issues in local government finance: the business occupancy tax; and exemptions from property taxes.

Business occupancy tax

The business occupancy tax is a significant source of revenue for Ontario municipalities and school boards, totalling some $1.5 billion annually in 1991. Business occupancy taxes account for approximately 12 per cent of all property taxes collected by municipalities for education and municipal purposes.

The most notable features of the business occupancy tax are its rate structure and the fact that it applies to the tenant in a commercial or industrial property rather than the owner.

The rate structure of the tax is an anachronism. The tax is levied as a percentage of the non-residential property taxes payable on the property occupied by the business. There are five tax rates ranging from 25 per cent to 75 per cent, depending on the type of business. The rates are based on a curious combination of what might have appeared to be ability to pay in 1904 when the rates were established and prohibitionist sentiments – the highest rates are reserved for breweries and distilleries.

"The concepts that were relevant in 1904 don't work any more. We're lost in time."
~ Hearings participant, London

We believe that the basic structure and purpose of the business occupancy tax cannot be justified on fairness grounds. While the tax may have been consistent with the social views and perceptions of ability to pay of the times when it was introduced in 1904, there is no rational basis for its structure today.

We recommend that the business occupancy tax be abolished and that municipalities be authorized to replace the revenue forgone from either residential or non-residential taxes.

To replace the current allowances in the property tax and business occupancy tax for unoccupied commercial and industrial property, we recommend that all property taxes on unoccupied commercial and industrial property be discounted by 40 per cent.

Exemptions

Our report presents an extensive review of the exemptions currently permitted from property taxes in Ontario.

Based in part on our view of tax exemptions generally and in part on our redefinition of the local property tax as a benefit tax for local services, we recommend that substantially all the exemptions for privately owned property currently provided for in various pieces of provincial legislation and private bills be eliminated. Exemptions for public property would be retained, but property owned by the provincial and federal governments or their agencies would be subject to full payment in lieu of local property taxes.

To ensure that treatment is consistent across the province, only the provincial government would have the authority to exempt property from local property taxation. Municipalities would, of course, retain the authority to provide grants for any local purpose, including offsetting their own property taxes.

Three areas are of particular interest: the taxation of "property held in trust for a band or body of Indians"; the taxation of charitable organizations; and the taxation of churches and cemeteries.

We recommend that the exemption for property held in trust for a band or body of Indians be restricted to reserve lands and other lands for which municipal services are not provided. Consistent with our view of the local property tax as a benefit tax for local services, our view would be that if a property benefits from locally provided services, it should be subject to tax.

We recommend that the exemptions for churches, cemeteries, religious and educational seminaries, and charitable organizations be eliminated. Churches and cemeteries should be assessed at standard unit rates rather than on the basis of their value in current use.

We recognize that our recommendation that charitable organizations and churches be subject to local property tax will be controversial. However, the impact of an end to existing exemptions to these types of properties will be significantly cushioned by other recommendations. The recommended change in the basis of assessment from market value to value in current use will reduce the relative assessed values of many properties owned by churches and charitable organizations, particularly in urban and urban fringe areas.

For churches and cemeteries, we have gone further and recommended that statutory unit rates of assessment be established in lieu of attempting to measure the value in current use of church sanctuaries and cemetery plots. Most important, our recommendation that local non-residential property taxes for education be eliminated will reduce by more than half the property taxes that would otherwise be paid by charitable organizations and churches, since these organizations would be exempt from the provincial commercial and industrial property tax on the grounds that they do not engage in a commercial activity.

Our recommendations are conditional in two respects. First, these changes would only be appropriate in an assessment system based on value in current use. Second, an extended notice and transitional period is essential to permit organizations affected by this change to adjust.

Technical exemptions

We also recommend changes in a number of technical exemptions, most notably in the taxation of underground mining facilities. The general rule we adopt is that any building, machinery, or equipment that would be taxable if it was located on the surface should be taxable if it is located underground.

PROVINCIAL PROPERTY TAXATION

Having decided to eliminate the local education levy on non-residential property and provide the core funding for education from provincial general revenues, we had to consider how to generate the additional revenue required at the provincial level.

Property taxes are essentially unrelated to the level of activity in a business and bear no relationship to its ability to generate revenue to pay the tax. This suggests that the mix of taxes on business should be shifted away from property taxes towards other taxes better related to business activity.

While the arguments in favour of reducing commercial and industrial property taxes are based on principles of taxation policy and local finance with which we have considerable sympathy, practical considerations led us to a different conclusion.

The local education portion of the non-residential property tax raises a substantial amount of revenue – nearly $3 billion in 1993. Only two taxes on business raise even close to that amount of revenue: the corporate income tax and the payroll tax. Given current economic circumstances, neither of these tax bases is capable of generating the additional revenue that would be required.

To generate the additional revenue required to meet the province's responsibility for funding primary and secondary education implied by our recommendations on education finance, Ontario requires a new provincial tax on commercial and industrial property.

Impact of a provincial commercial and industrial property tax

A provincial tax on commercial and industrial property would have to be levied at the same effective rate across Ontario. Different rates of tax would be very difficult to justify as a permanent feature of the system.

The effective rate of tax currently levied for education at the local level on non-residential property varies dramatically among municipalities. There are a number of reasons for these variations.

First, average rates of business occupancy taxation vary among municipalities. A uniform tax rate that eliminates the business occupancy tax portion of taxes on business for education purposes would replace a variety of different average rates of tax with a single tax rate.

Second, differences in assessment practices across the province lead to dramatically different effective tax rates on non-residential property across the province. A uniform provincial tax would wipe out those differences.

Third, spending levels on education vary across Ontario and produce a corresponding variety of tax rates for education on non-residential property. These differences would not be reflected in a provincial tax.

The replacement of the current range of effective tax rates with a single uniform rate would create significant tax shifts both between geographical areas and between different types of commercial and industrial property in the same area.

Businesses in some municipalities will experience tax increases. In other municipalities businesses will experience tax decreases. Impacts will also differ between commercial and industrial properties. Industrial properties will, generally speaking, experience larger decreases and smaller increases than commercial properties.

Shifts in taxation of this magnitude cannot be absorbed easily or immediately. Special transitional arrangements will be necessary to provide affected taxpayers with an opportunity to adjust to these shifts.

We recommend that the change from current levels of taxation for education at the local level to a uniform provincial rate of tax be phased in over a period of five years.

Assessment

The proposed provincial commercial and industrial tax would be levied on the assessed value of commercial and industrial property as established for municipal taxation purposes and equalized to a common base across Ontario.

The arguments which convinced us that market value assessment does not work in the local property tax system apply here, too. If a provincial commercial and industrial tax is to play a role as a tax on business, the base of the tax should be measured by the value of the property in its current use or rental value, rather than its

FIGURE 13
IMPACT ON TOTAL COMMERCIAL AND INDUSTRIAL TAXES OF UNIFORM COMMERCIAL AND INDUSTRIAL RATE FOR EDUCATION, ONTARIO, 1991

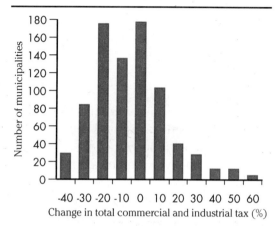

Source: Fair Tax Commission calculations based on Ontario, Ministry of Municipal Affairs, Municipal Analysis and Retrieval System (MARS).

Note: Figure shows the distribution of impacts on total commercial and industrial taxes of changing to a uniform rate for the education portion of the tax, by municipality.

market value at arm's-length sale. Value in current use will generally be a better reflection of current business activity than market value because it is not distorted by values attributable to potential future uses or potential future capital gains or losses.

To the extent that an incremental value attributable to a future change of use may be seen as a business activity measure, that value should be subject to tax when it is realized, through such measures as the capital gains tax or a special tax on land value increments.

As a practical matter, if non-residential property is already being assessed on the basis of value in current use for the local non-residential property tax, it would make sense to use the same tax base for those properties that are subject to the proposed provincial commercial and industrial tax.

Provincial Property Tax

Rate structure

The rate structure for the proposed provincial commercial and industrial tax should be set to generate approximately the same amount of revenue that the business occupancy tax and the non-residential property tax currently raise for education at the local level.

Exemptions

The proposed provincial commercial and industrial property tax should apply to all non-residential property used for a business purpose. Property owned by a non-profit organization and used for a non-profit or charitable purpose should be exempt.

Exemptions from a provincial tax on business activity with property as the base would be much broader than those that we recommend for local non-residential property tax. In principle, since the purpose of the tax is to tax business, property that is not owned by a business or used for a business purpose should be exempt from the tax.

Farming property

As we noted in our discussion of local property taxes, all farming property other than the principal residence and one acre of land should, in principle, be subject to provincial commercial and industrial property taxation.

Taxation of farm land cannot, however, be addressed fully with reference only to property taxes. In the current system for education funding, the Farm Tax Rebate program is intended to compensate farmers for the education portion of the local property tax. The rebate is equivalent to an exemption from education property taxes on farming property (other than the farm residence).

"The Farm Tax Rebate is not a subsidy. It represents money that should not have been collected in the first place since it is compensation for overpayment of education." ~ Hearings participant, Thunder Bay

This gives rise to two policy issues. Should farming property continue to be cushioned from the impact of property taxes other than those required for local municipal services? If so, should this assistance be delivered in the form of a rebate similar to the Farm Tax Rebate, or should it be in the form of an exemption from the tax?

A decision not to cushion farming property from the impact of our proposed provincial commercial and industrial property would single out the farming industry for significant tax increases. A reduction in net support for the farming industry of the size implied by the application of our proposed provincial commercial and industrial property tax to farming property could only be contemplated in the context of a much broader evaluation of the economics of the farming industry. Such an evaluation goes beyond our mandate. We recommend, therefore, that farming property be exempt from provincial commercial and industrial property taxation, and, accordingly, that the Farm Tax Rebate program be eliminated.

A NEW TAX MIX DESIGN

We considered four tax sources (and combinations of them) to replace the residential property tax currently used to fund education and some social services. These sources were the provincial payroll tax, the corporate income tax, the retail sales tax, and the personal income tax.

The net decrease in residential property taxes which the provincial government would have to make up from other sources would be $3.5 billion. The residential property tax related to the funding of education and social services amounts to $4.6 billion in 1993. The local levy we recommend to support particular education programs supplemented to provincially funded programs could generate about $727 million annually (about 5 per cent of total spending).

Our recommended changes in the system of grants to municipal governments would result in a decrease in grants. Local governments would presumably recoup these moneys from their own property tax bases, with about $373 million coming from the residential tax base.

The payroll tax offers considerable potential for additional revenues. A relatively modest increase in the rate could generate substantial amounts of revenue because the base of this tax – all wages and salaries – is broad. Further, compared with the Quebec and many non-Canadian jurisdictions, Ontario's current payroll tax rate is low, and in this sense there is room to increase reliance on this tax.

However, we have already concluded that the payroll tax, in the long run, is borne by employees. That is of concern to us because the incidence of the tax is not particularly progressive. A tax such as an income tax, which falls on all sources of income, not just labour, is more progressive. This is one of the reasons we decided that we were not prepared to recommend that reliance on the payroll tax be increased to the extent required (at least doubled) to offset the property tax reduction.

We also determined that the corporate income tax could not be the source for this additional revenue, but for a different reason. While the decision not to increase the payroll tax in the overall tax mix was a matter of choice, the decision with respect to the corporate income tax reflects a judgment about constraints. Given the mobility of the tax base and of capital itself, an attempt to increase the tax rate to the extent required to generate a significant portion of the required revenues would be self-defeating. In our view, debates about the desirability of heavier taxes on the corporate sector are almost beside the point, since increased corporate taxes are unfeasible, particularly for a subnational jurisdiction such as Ontario.

A New Tax
Mix Design

We are left with a choice between the personal income tax and the retail sales tax. Increasing revenues from each or from a combination of the two is, in our opinion, feasible. There is room to increase the retail sales tax rate. The current rate in Ontario is below that of several other provinces and, with implementation of the reforms we recommend for the tax, it would be able to generate significantly more in revenue than it currently does.

There is also room to generate more revenue from the personal income tax. Taking into account the disincentive and potential mobility consequences of higher income tax rates, it is possible to design a tax rate schedule that will include more brackets than exist in the current system, with graduated rates throughout, and to maintain the combined federal and provincial marginal rate on the highest income bracket at less than 60 per cent. Given these two alternatives, we opt for increased income taxes in preference to higher sales taxes. Even alongside all the structural reforms we recommend for other taxes, the income tax is a fairer way to raise the required revenue. It is clearly more progressive than the sales tax, and for that reason advances our objective of a tax system that more clearly reflects ability-to-pay principles.

With small amounts of additional revenue generated as a result of our recommendations concerning the structure of the retail sales tax ($300 million), the payroll tax ($150 million), and the corporate income tax ($50 million), the net amount that would have to be generated from increased personal income tax revenues would be $3 billion. We are not including any revenue gain from the elimination of the capital gains exemption because it is doubtful that recent values for the tax

expenditure are representative of the likely experience over a longer period of time. A high percentage of taxpayers with capital gains have already taken advantage of the exemption.

We recommend that the provincial government meet its additional requirement as follows:

Residential ($ billions)

Education property taxes	4.600	
LESS Local levy	0.727	
Grants offset (net)	0.373	
Property tax reduction		**3.500**

To be replaced by

PIT rate changes	3.000
Sales tax base	0.300
Payroll tax changes	0.150
Corporate income tax uniform rate	0.050
Additional revenue	**3.500**

Commercial and industrial ($ billions)

Education property taxes	3.095	
LESS Grants offset (net)	0.251	
Local property tax change		**2.844**

To be replaced by

Provincial commercial and industrial tax	**2.844**

On the assumption that the Tax Collection Agreements are amended along the lines we recommend, we have designed a schedule of income tax brackets and rates that would meet the requirement recommended above and, at the same time, incorporate the proposed child and adult credits as replacements for the sales and property tax credits.

A New Tax
Mix Design

Obviously, other combinations of rate schedules and refundable credits would also meet the revenue target we have established. There is nothing absolute about the schedules we propose below. For example, with higher tax rates it would be possible to afford larger refundable credits than those we recommend. In addition, if tax credit reforms are considered along with reforms to the social assistance system, shifts between direct assistance and tax benefit programs can be considered. However, working with the resources currently available in the tax system, it is our view that our recommendations are consistent with the principles we have established.

Assuming Ontario is able to establish an independent rate structure and credit system for its personal income tax, the following rate schedule and credit would generate sufficient additional revenue to meet the requirements flowing from the elimination of the residential property tax:

Rate schedule

Taxable income ($)	Marginal rate (%)
10,000 and under	10
10,001–20,000	12
20,001–29,590	14
29,591–40,000	16
40,001–50,000	18
50,001–59,180	20
59,181–80,000	22
80,001–150,000	24
150,001–250,000	26
Over 250,000	28

- A basic personal non-refundable credit with the amount claimed equal to the federal amount and the credit rate equal to the lowest Ontario marginal tax rate.

Refundable credit amounts would be as follows:

- an Ontario tax assistance credit of $500 per adult family member up to family income of $18,000, and reduced at a rate of 8.3 per cent of income in excess of $18,000;

- an additional Ontario tax assistance credit of $300 for individuals aged 65 and over;

- a child tax credit of $600 for the first child and $500 for each additional child, up to a family income of $18,000, and reduced at a rate of 7.5 per cent of income in excess of $18,000;

- an additional credit of $400 for the first child in a single parent family.

The adult and seniors credits would apply to individuals not in families on the same basis as they apply to families.

If Ontario establishes an income-tested child benefit that provides benefits to families with children regardless of the family's source of income, the child tax benefit should be eliminated and folded into this new program.

This recommended tax mix is designed to be revenue neutral compared with the current Ontario system. It does not take into account any tax changes requiring implementation at the federal level. Some changes are potentially large enough to affect Ontario's revenues to the extent that the tax mix issue would need to be revisited. These involve the changes to the taxation of capital income in the income tax

A New Tax Mix Design

(capital gains, dividends), the treatment of contributions to pension plans and RRSPs, and the introduction of a wealth transfer tax. Definitive recommendations on tax mix following these changes would depend on the revenue implications for Ontario.

However, we believe that in the first instance the revenues from these additional reforms should be used to bring down personal income tax rates. Most of these changes would result in higher income tax revenues. Accordingly, compensating rate adjustments would be appropriate.

A New Tax
Mix Design

ABORIGINAL PEOPLE AND TAXATION IN ONTARIO

After years of discussion, the issue of aboriginal self-government has begun to receive serious consideration from both the provincial government and the federal government. In 1991 the Ontario government negotiated a statement of relationship between the province and aboriginal peoples that acknowledged self-government as a legitimate goal of First Nation communities. Constitutional recognition of the right to aboriginal self-government was also included as part of the package of constitutional reforms negotiated by the provincial governments and the federal government and put to the electorate in 1992 in a referendum. While the defeat of the proposed package of reforms in the Charlottetown accord has clearly put formal constitutional recognition of the right to self-government on hold, discussions continue between governments and aboriginal communities on issues of self-government.

The emergence of aboriginal self-government will likely give rise to a number of taxation issues involving both the aboriginal governments and the government of Ontario. Currently, however, attention tends to focus on disputes and grievances relating to the interpretation and administration of the aboriginal tax status.

Status Indians are exempt from paying property tax on reserves; from sales tax and from many excise taxes on products to be consumed on a reserve; and from income tax when the income is deemed to have originated on a reserve. The administration and interpretation of the breadth of the exemption is complicated by the absence of a consensus on why the exemption or the immunity exists.

Many non-aboriginal people assume that the exemption is simply another tax expenditure intended to assist economic development in reserve communities. They claim it should be evaluated according to its success in achieving these goals, and, if found wanting, it should be changed or abolished. Others accept the argument that the exemption is a right of some sort, but interpret it very narrowly. They see the exemption as being rigidly limited to the reserve.

Clearly, from the aboriginal perspective of taxation immunity, the economic development rationale is the wrong focus for explaining their status. They argue that they are a sovereign people within Canada, and are therefore immune from taxation by all Canadian governments.

The current disputes and grievances tend to capture most of the headlines. While these disputes raise important issues, in general they are not issues of tax fairness. The only such issue with which we deal in our report is that of municipal taxation of off-reserve property, where we argue that the benefit tax framework for local

Aboriginal
People and Tax

property taxes requires that such property be taxed if it benefits from local services.

However, another taxation issue will soon require the attention of aboriginal leaders and the provincial government. This issue relates to the emergence of First Nations self-government arrangements.

Indian governments will, of course, continue to receive funding from the federal (and to a lesser extent the provincial) government, and for most communities these grants will constitute the majority of their public resources. However, if Indian governments are to succeed, it will be necessary for them to develop their own taxation sources as well.

As is the case with other governments exercising autonomy over particular areas, Indian governments could in principle tax their own citizens and non-residents with interests on Indian lands. The existence of Indian government tax regimes will require that protocols be developed to coordinate their operation with the tax systems of the provincial and other non-aboriginal governments. Clearly one would want to avoid outcomes such as double taxation on the one hand, and, on the other, the complete avoidance of taxation because of reporting gaps.

If Indian governments intend to levy taxes on these bases, tax harmonization agreements will be required with the federal or provincial government that already administers a comparable tax. In these cases the federal-provincial Tax Collection Agreements (TCAs) and allocation agreements become a useful model for aboriginal taxation. The principle that should be adopted from the TCAs is the recognition by each government of the taxing authority of the other, and the commitment implied in that recognition to coordinate tax systems where required.

In this context, there are two aspects to tax coordination. First, where an aboriginal government chooses to enter a tax field, the provincial and local governments should recognize that initiative and adjust accordingly. Second, where direct aboriginal taxation is not feasible, but there is still a desire by an aboriginal government to access the tax base, the province should be prepared to negotiate an administrative agreement to bring this into effect.

Clarification of the taxing authority of First Nation governments, and the recognition of this authority by other governments, can facilitate the aboriginal self-government process. In addition, it can help to resolve many current tax disputes. Further, the readiness of Ontario to assist First Nation governments in the development of administrative mechanisms to enable them to collect their own taxes where feasible, and to collect taxes on their behalf in other areas, would be a concrete statement of goodwill and support to First Nation governments. While it is premature to specify details, we believe that a statement by the Ontario government indicating its willingness to work towards such arrangements is warranted.

Aboriginal People and Tax

IMPACT, IMPLICATIONS, AND TRANSITION

 Impact of our recommendations

In formulating our recommendations we were most concerned with two types of impact. First, we wanted to change the distribution of taxes among Ontarians to bring about greater fairness and to make the system more progressive. Second, we wanted to ensure that the reconfigured tax system would not have negative effects on the economy.

Impact on tax fairness

If our recommendations are implemented, the combined tax revenue collected by the provincial and local governments would remain the same. The impact of these proposed changes would be significantly progressive. They would reduce the combined amount of income tax, property tax, and sales tax paid by families with income up to about $40,000, and they would increase the amount of tax paid by families with incomes above $50,000. Homeowners would experience these changes through reductions in property taxes; tenants through reductions in residential rents.

The largest single tax change we are proposing is to reduce the residential property tax by $3.5 billion. Approximately $3 billion of this amount would be shifted to the personal income tax and the remainder

TABLE 4
ESTIMATED IMPACT OF PROPOSED CHANGES TO INCOME, PROPERTY, AND SALES TAXES, 1993 (CENSUS FAMILIES)

Total income group ($)	Total Ontario tax impact ($ millions)	Average dollar impact ($)	% change in disposable income
10,000 & under	236	580	9.6
10,001–20,000	641	690	4.9
20,001–30,000	290	440	1.9
30,001–40,000	21	40	0.1
40,001–50,000	-9	-20	-0.1
50,001–60,000	-35	-90	-0.2
60,001–70,000	-39	-130	-0.2
70,001–90,000	-25	-70	-0.1
Over 90,000	-887	-1950	-1.6
Total	192[a]	40	0.1

Source: Fair Tax Commission estimates based on Statistics Canada Social Policy Simulation Database and Model (SPSD/M).

a. Overall amount of tax to be raised through recommended changes to other taxes.

Note: Negative sign indicates decline in disposable income/increase in tax; otherwise indicates increase in disposable income/decline in tax.

would be generated by changes to the retail sales tax, payroll tax, as well as through other smaller tax changes. The higher levels of income tax will of course be offset by the reduction in the property tax burden faced by residents in Ontario as a result of the tax

Impact, Implications, and Transition

mix change. Because the property tax is regressive and the income tax system is progressive, the combined effect of these changes will be to shift the burden of taxation from people with lower and middle-range incomes towards people with higher incomes and a greater ability to pay.

The new personal income tax rate structure that we have recommended is an important component of this restructured tax mix. In recommending this change in rate structure, we are guided by the desire to ensure that middle-income earners do not face an increase in their marginal tax rates (the rate they pay on an additional dollar of income). The effective Ontario marginal tax rate currently is 22 per cent at income of about $63,000. The new tax structure we propose would keep the same rate for those with incomes between $59,180 and $80,000.

The following calculations do not take into account our recommendations for the treatment of dividends, capital gains, and a national wealth tax.

Families with income below $10,000 would experience an average reduction of $580 in the taxes they pay each year.

This decline would result in a 10 per cent increase in their disposable income.

Families with income in the $10,000 to $20,000 range would experience an average decline of $690 in the amount of tax they pay annually.

This would result in a 5 per cent increase in their disposable income. These decreases in taxes paid and increases in disposable income are significant for these low-income families.

Families in the middle-income ranges, $40,000 to $90,000, would experience minor changes in the amount of tax they pay and in their disposable income. Families with incomes over $90,000 (aver-

age income for this group is about $150,000) would pay on average an extra $1950 in tax, representing a 1.6 per cent decline in disposable income.

Single parents as a group would derive the greatest benefit from these tax changes.

On average, single parents in Ontario would experience a decrease in their tax burden of $680 per year, increasing their disposable income by 2.2 per cent. The tax and credit changes for single parents with income of less than $20,000, almost all of whom are women, would, on average, result in an increase in after-tax income of approximately $1500 per year. For single parents with income in the $10,000 to $20,000 range, this means an 11 per cent increase in disposable income. Given the high rate of poverty among single parents and the importance attached to reducing child poverty, this outcome is highly desirable.

Low-income couples with children would also experience a large reduction in the taxes they pay and a corresponding increase in their disposable income.

The reduction in the overall tax burden for couples with children affects all income classes except those with income over $90,000.

Unattached elderly individuals as a group are net beneficiaries.

Single elderly people at the lowest income levels – below $20,000 – would experience an increase in disposable income, but those with incomes above $20,000 would experience an increase in their taxes and small percentage declines in disposable income.

The package of recommended changes would contribute to the alleviation of poverty in Ontario.

We used as our measure of poverty the low-income cut-offs produced by Statistics Canada. The low-income cut-off defines

Impact, Implications, and Transition

low income as the level of income below which most of a family's income must be spent on essentials.

If our proposed changes had been in place in 1993, the percentage of families below the low-income cut-off, which varies with family size and the population level in the community where the family resides, would have been about 1 per cent lower. This figure represents a decrease of about 50,000 in the number of Ontario families below the low-income cut-off, about 7 per cent of the current total. The largest proportional improvement occurs among single parent families; the incidence of poverty for this group declines by more than 2 per cent.

Impact on the economy

In formulating our recommendations to increase the fairness of the tax system in Ontario, we were aware of the need to consider their economic impact. We analysed the impact of our recommendations on the Ontario economy from 1995 until 2001. Overall, the recommendations that were modelled have a marginally positive impact — right through to 2001 — on the Ontario economy, the Ontario labour market, and the Ontario government's fiscal position, in particular the provincial debt.

In real terms – that is, after factoring out inflation – the gross provincial product would be higher than the level otherwise projected by 0.3 per cent in 1995, by 0.5 per cent in 1996, by 0.7 per cent in 1997, and then by 0.8 per cent in the years 1998 to 2001. The unemployment rate is predicted to be between 0.1 and 0.2 percentage points lower than it would be without our recommended changes, and labour productivity is predicted to be higher, although by less than 1 per cent.

With our recommended changes to the tax mix, the tax system would generate the same amount of revenue as it does now. However, the economic growth that is predicted as a result of our recommendations is assumed to lead to increases in the Ontario government's tax revenue. The deficit would be $600 million lower than otherwise expected by 2001. As a result of the reduction in property taxes, there would be a one-time reduction of 1.1 percentage points in the rate of inflation in 1995 and additional marginal reductions in subsequent years.

Implications for intergovernmental relations

Ontario's role as a subnational jurisdiction in a federal structure, along with its constitutional responsibility for local government, places it in the middle of a complex web of relationships among the three orders of government.

Because these relationships are to a significant degree fiscal, they both affect and are affected by provincial tax and revenue reform proposals. The impact of these fiscal relationships is considered throughout our report. Ontario's relationship with the federal government and Ontario's role in the Canadian economy more generally have had a profound impact on our recommendations in every major tax area. And, to a significant degree, our proposals for local government finance reform are in fact about the provincial/local fiscal relationship.

Implications for local government

Our research and our public consultations suggest that the structure of local government – both for education and for municipal services – is in need of renewal. The additional pressures on that structure posed by the financial reforms we recommend should be welcomed as opening up new opportunities to make progress towards that end. The alternative, allowing opposition

Impact, Implications, and Transition

from the existing institutional structure to block any attempt at reform, will perpetuate the gross unfairness of the existing system.

School boards

Our recommendations on the financing of education would transform the financial base for elementary and secondary education in Ontario. Locally determined property taxes currently account for approximately 60 per cent of educational costs on average across the province. Taken together, our recommendations would reduce that share dramatically. Commercial and industrial property taxes and business occupancy taxes currently levied at the local level for school board purposes would be replaced by a provincial tax levied at a uniform rate across the province. The local levy on residential property for education would be limited, probably to no more than 10 per cent of total education spending. Assuming that, overall, half the potential local levy of approximately $1.4 billion is actually exercised by local school boards, residential taxes for education would be, on average, approximately 16 per cent of their current level.

In our hearings and in other consultations with the public, the only consistent objection to the idea of shifting the funding base for education from local property taxes to provincial revenue sources concerned the potential impact of such a move on the effectiveness of school boards as local democratic institutions. School trustees and other active participants in the education governance system argued that the elimination of local funding for education would make the system unresponsive to local conditions. They pointed out that school boards, if they cease to be responsible for levying taxes for most of their spending, will no longer be accountable to their electorates for their actions.

We believe our recommendations concerning education finance could serve as a catalyst, eliminating some of the obstacles that might otherwise stand in the way of education governance reform. If the financial resources available to a particular school no longer depend on the local property tax base to which the board responsible for the school has access, the concerns about the potential impact of governance reform on the resources available for education funding cease to be a factor.

With the local tax contribution reduced to this extent, alternatives to the municipal model of education governance may become more attractive.

For example, options such as a combination of school-based and region-based governance that have been implemented in a number of jurisdictions in the Organisation for Economic Co-operation and Development make a lot more sense if the funding base does not require a municipal approach. We explore some of the implications and options of these approaches in our report, not to suggest that they are necessarily appropriate for Ontario, but to illustrate the kinds of options that financing reform might open up.

At the same time, we recognize that governance reform is constrained by factors other than finances. The most important limiting factors relate to the constitutionally protected identities of public and separate school boards, as well as English- and French-language school boards. In addition, schools are an important part of the fabric of a community, and are of considerable interest to those involved in community planning and development. Any new approach to governance must accommodate a connection to that process. Schools also play an important role in the delivery of programs in areas other than education. Again, any governance model must either accommodate that role or ensure that it is played appropriately elsewhere in the system.

Municipal government

Our recommendations call for a system of local government finance in Ontario in which municipal governments exercise increased power over taxation policy. They would wield this authority within a provincial policy framework that is clearly defined and rooted specifically in principles of tax fairness.

Our proposed municipal financial system would recognize the fact that the property tax is actually two taxes: a tax on the housing occupied by residents of the municipality; and a tax on property used by businesses operating in the municipality. Municipalities would have the power, within broad limits, to exercise taxation policy by establishing rates for each of these taxes independently of each other. We also propose that municipalities rely much more heavily on user charges for sewer, water, and solid waste services.

Our recommendations with respect to provincial grants policy and the allocation of financial responsibility for programs between the provincial government and the municipal governments follow the same direction as our proposals for education finance reform. In particular, we recommend that the provincial government continue with its reform of social assistance financing and assume full responsibility for financing of services to children. We also propose that the province reduce its grants to municipal governments for services of local benefit by $700 million (for a net impact of $624 million after allowing for provincial assumption of full funding for children's services).

The limited success of the Provincial/Local Relationship Review (the recent provincial initiative known as disentangle- ment, abandoned in 1993) in arriving at trade-offs between financial and program responsibilities underlines the difficulties in achieving reform in this area.

We believe, however, that the approach we recommend could give significant new impetus to this area of reform because it responds to a number of the lessons from that experience. First, reform of the local government finance system is impossible unless education finance issues are addressed at the same time. Because education currently accounts for more than half of property taxes, reforms that address only the municipal side are addressing less than half the issue, as it is perceived by taxpayers. Second, revenue reform must proceed in tandem with expenditure reform. Not all the problems of local government finance are on the expenditure side. As a result, meaningful reform cannot take place on a revenue-neutral basis. Third, reform cannot be successful if it proceeds on the assumption, either implied or explicit, that all local governments are the same. Local governments are extremely diverse, with vastly different administrative and political capabilities, and they have different capacities to participate in a reformed financial and administrative structure.

Implications for federal/provincial relations

In the course of our work, we identified many areas in which our recommendations bear on the relationship between Ontario and the federal government. In some areas, our recommendations call for an expansion of the provincial role set out in federal-provincial agreements. In other areas, we address potential benefits from increased harmonization of provincial and federal taxation policies. In still other areas, we make recommendations for

Impact, Implications, and Transition

changes in federal tax policy, in recognition of the fact that action by Ontario on its own would be impractical or undesirable.

There are four major areas in which our recommendations involve the federal government. First, a number of recommendations involving the personal income tax require the federal government to change its income tax. For Ontario to take action by itself would be either administratively unfeasible or self-defeating, in the sense that taxpayers could easily arrange their affairs to take advantage of provisions that were more favourable at the federal (and other provincial) level. These provisions include the treatment of the capital gains exclusion and dividends, the taxation of alimony and child support payments, and tax support for registered pension plan and RRSP contributions. Another set of recommendations depends on Ontario gaining greater control over its income tax policy. This can only be accomplished through renegotiation of federal-provincial Tax Collection Agreements.

Second, we conclude that attempts to use the provincial corporate income tax to accomplish economic policy goals different from those inherent in the corresponding federal tax are unlikely to be sufficiently effective to justify their revenue costs and the added complexity and compliance costs for corporate taxpayers.

Third, we recommend that the Ontario retail sales tax be coordinated, in concert with other provinces, with a revised version of the federal Goods and Services Tax.

Finally, we recommend a wealth transfer tax on the basis that it would make a significant contribution to a fairer tax system, but conclude that potential problems of compliance require that an effective wealth tax be implemented only at the national level.

Federal/provincial fiscal relations

Our recommendations, if implemented, would increase the degree of harmonization in the tax system between the federal and the provincial governments. We would not recommend, however, that these changes be negotiated in isolation from the broader context of federal/provincial fiscal relations.

The recent history of federal grants to the provinces is not encouraging, at least from the perspective of provinces such as Ontario.

The federal government, through the Canada Assistance Plan (CAP), has traditionally paid 50 per cent of each province's welfare costs (provided assistance is available on the basis of need and that no residence requirement is imposed as a condition). In 1990 a 5 per cent limit was imposed on annual increases in CAP transfers to each of the "have" provinces – Alberta, British Columbia, and Ontario. This ceiling came into effect as Ontario plunged into a severe recession. The fiscal consequences have been grim. The federal share of social assistance expenditures in Ontario fell from 50 per cent as recently as 1989–90, to 28 per cent in 1992–93, representing a revenue loss of $1.8 billion.

The federal government introduced limits to the Established Programs Financing (a program that indirectly supports post-secondary education and health care) in 1983, and several times thereafter. Finally, in 1989, increases were frozen for four years. The combined effect of these federal cutbacks cost Ontario an estimated $2.7 billion in 1992–93.

If closer tax cooperation is to emerge between the federal government and the provinces, with revenue balances adjusted even partially through grant programs, it is essential that the provinces have reason to have more confidence in the stability of these grants. Although it is beyond our purview to provide specific recommendations, it is important to point out that progress in the area of tax coordination cannot proceed without addressing these broader components of fiscal federalism as well.

Implementation and transition

Our recommendations for fair tax reform touch on virtually every aspect of taxation in this province.

The central recommendations of our report will have a significant impact on the kinds of taxes people pay, on the way those taxes are distributed among individual taxpayers, and on the relationships between the provincial government and both local governments and the federal government.

Implementation of our key recommendations for education finance reform and for a more progressive mix of taxes in Ontario will result in a shift of approximately $3.5 billion from residential property taxes to other taxes, primarily the personal income tax.

Replacement of local non-residential property taxation for education purposes with a provincial commercial and industrial property tax levied at a uniform rate across the province will result in substantial tax increases in some areas and substantial tax decreases in others as we replace a system of taxation that is fundamentally irrational.

Assessment reform in both the residential and the non-residential sectors will give rise to shifts in taxation within municipalities, as properties that have been undertaxed relative to their value in current use see tax increases and properties that have been overtaxed see tax reductions.

Education finance reform in particular and local government finance reform in general beg important questions about the relationship between the provincial government and our institutions of local government.

Transition and fairness

While we do not believe that the old maxim "an old tax is a good tax" can be taken as an excuse for inaction in the face of unfairness, transition itself raises fairness issues. First, fairness in transition is an important element of fairness in taxation. In our economy, people and institutions are constantly adjusting to change. Those adjustments are not always easy, nor do they take place without cost. The bigger the change that must be absorbed, the more difficult the adjustment will be. To be implemented fairly, tax reform must give taxpayers adequate notice of the change and enough time to adjust their financial affairs to take its impact into account.

> "The commission must make recommendations that are possible to implement. The taxation system has got to be simpler."
> ~ Hearings participant, Peterborough

Second, as a practical matter, a reform that does not address issues arising from transition cannot be implemented successfully. Without careful emphasis on transitional issues from the beginning, it is difficult to shift the debate over tax reform initiatives from the immediate impact on individual taxpayers or interest groups to the fairness principles that are advanced by the reforms.

Third, many of the recommendations put forward in our report will enhance the fairness of the tax system as a whole only if they are implemented in coordination with other recommendations.

Specific implementation issues

The three areas in which implementation and transition challenges are the greatest involve negotiations with the federal government, education finance, and property assessment.

Impact, Implications, and Transition

Federal/provincial policy changes

The provincial government should develop a coordinated strategy for negotiating with the federal government for changes in the personal income tax collection agreement; reforms in the tax treatment of child support and alimony; taxation of dividends and capital gains; the tax treatment of Registered Retirement Savings Plans and private pensions; sales tax harmonization; wealth transfer taxation; and a framework agreement on the income tax treatment of federal, provincial, and local taxes paid by corporations.

Education finance

Our recommendations with respect to education are the most sensitive and the most carefully balanced of all our recommendations dealing with local government finance. It is essential, therefore, that our recommendations be considered and implemented as an interrelated package. In particular, our recommendation for a funding allocation model based on cost and student needs must be implemented at the same time as our recommendations for an end to funding education through local property taxes.

Implementation of revenue reform without funding allocation reform would lead to the conclusion that the reform initiative was little more than a disguised version of commercial and industrial assessment pooling. Proceeding on the expenditure side without addressing the fairness issues on the revenue side would be interpreted as a provincial power grab combined with further downloading of costs onto local governments.

It is also important that other elements of the local government finance reform package be in place to facilitate the change in education funding and to ensure that it achieves its fairness objectives. The authority for municipal governments to levy tax rates separately on residential and non-residential property is an essential part of the

package, as is our recommendation for a mechanism to ensure that property tax reductions are passed through to tenants.

Property tax and assessment reform

Both assessment reform and the change from a local non-residential tax for education to a provincial tax at a uniform rate will produce tax shifts for individual taxpayers. Some of these shifts will be significant. Although the irrationality of the existing system makes tax shifts inevitable, such shifts call for special transitional measures to cushion the impact.

In our view, the best way to cushion the impact of these tax changes is to spread them out over a number of years. It is important, however, that transition take place over a defined period of time and that all taxpayers be treated in the same way. Transitional arrangements that are linked to the sale of property, for example, are unfair. They are also likely to result in a transitional period that never ends.

We recommend that transition take place over a period of five years, with taxes shifting from the old base to the new base step by step over that period.

Coordinating the provincial response

Local government finance reform involves the interests of a large number of the current provincial government ministries. A partial list includes the Ministries of Finance, Education and Training, Municipal Affairs, Transportation, Environment and Energy, and Community and Social Services. This complicates the development of a coherent response to broad issues of local government finance. To facilitate both the consideration of options for local government finance reform and the implementation of any changes that result, we recommend that the provincial government consolidate its resources for dealing with local government finance in a single ministry.

Impact, Implications, and Transition

APPENDIX A
RECOMMENDATIONS

Improving Accountability in the Tax System

1 Ontario should apply the rule of budget secrecy only to the details of tax changes that might enable an individual to derive financial gain through prior knowledge.

In general, the process of budget policy making should be carried out under the same restrictions as those applicable to other policy questions requiring cabinet decisions.

2 Public multi-group presentations to, and discussions with, the provincial minister of finance should be a regular part of the Ontario tax policy process and form the basis of Ontario's budget considerations. The list of participants and any formal presentations made in such discussions should be made public by the minister.

3 Ontario should establish a central agency responsible for:

- maintaining all government databases related to provincial or local public finance,
- ensuring consistency and comparability of those databases, and
- publishing information about public finance in Ontario.

Access to provincial data sources should be provided to outside researchers and the public, subject to the personal privacy provisions of the Access to Information Act and any federal/provincial agreements with respect to confidentiality.

4 Programs should be delivered through the tax system only if they satisfy the following criteria:

a) The rules for determining eligibility for the subsidy are so simple and easy to apply that application for the subsidy can be built into a tax-filing process based on self-assessment by taxpayers.

b) The program can be administered effectively by the Ministry of Finance rather than the government department normally responsible for the policy area.

c) There is a high degree of certainty the program will not be abused.

d) It is appropriate for the subsidy to be delivered on an infrequent basis in conjunction with the filing of tax returns and the payment of tax refunds.

e) Where monitoring and auditing are considered necessary, appropriate provisions are built into the design of the program.

f) The potential for costs to escalate in an open-ended program can be addressed effectively in the design of the tax expenditure program.

g) The tax expenditure program can be designed so that it does not affect the operation of the general rules governing the tax system.

If there is doubt as to whether a program should be delivered directly or through the tax sytem, it should be delivered directly.

5 To ensure that the benefits from tax expenditures in the income tax system do not increase with income, tax expenditures should be delivered in the form of a tax credit rather than a tax deduction.

To ensure that tax expenditures are fully equivalent to grants, they should generally be taxable. They should also generally be refundable and therefore paid whether or not the taxpayer has taxable income.

Recommendations

6 All tax expenditures should be dealt with in the government's budget-making process in the same way as direct spending programs designed to achieve the same objectives.

    a) Information on tax expenditures should be made available to pre-budget roundtables and consultations.

    b) The relevant government department should be involved in the design and review of each tax expenditure program.

7 a) Tax expenditure programs should be monitored to ensure that they continue to satisfy criteria for delivery through the tax system as opposed to the direct expenditure system.

    b) Ontario should include tax expenditures in annual program reviews. In addition, tax expenditures should be subject to periodic in-depth evaluations on a rotating basis on the same basis as expenditure programs.

    c) Legislation should be introduced to expand the authority of the provincial auditor to audit tax expenditures on a basis that mirrors the process for direct expenditures.

    d) Corporations should be required to disclose the benefits received from all tax expenditure provisions in the same way that benefits received from direct spending programs are disclosed.

    e) Ontario should publish an annual tax expenditure account. This account should include:
- the objectives of each tax expenditure;
- its statutory basis;
- an estimate of revenue forgone;
- a description of the relationship between the tax expenditure and corresponding direct expenditure programs; and
- summary tables showing the distribution of benefits from the tax expenditure among different categories of beneficiaries.

The purpose of the account is to draw attention to tax expenditures and encourage analysis of whether policy objectives are being met or whether other approaches would be more effective and efficient.

8 Ontario should earmark taxes for specific government programs only where:
- the benefits from the service can be attributed to individuals;
- redistribution is not an objective in providing the service;
- public policy does not require that the service be provided as a right;
- efficiency and public accountability would be enhanced; and
- there is a clear relationship between the earmarked fee or tax and the service to be funded.

Ontario should not create the impression that taxes are earmarked by using names that describe an expenditure program rather than the base of the tax. Ontario should therefore change the name of its Employer Health Tax.

Paying Other People's Taxes: Problems of Compliance

9 Ontario should seek the agreement of the federal government to establish and strictly enforce rules applicable to corporate expenditures which provide employees with personal benefits such as meals expenditures. Where possible, the personal element of such expenditures should be attributed as income to those who derive the private benefit.

Where it is not practical to attribute benefit to individuals, the corresponding deductions by the business incurring the expense should be limited.

The same limits should apply to business expense deductions, whether they are claimed by a corporation or by an individual claiming deductions from income from self-employment.

Ontario should seek the agreement of the federal government to disallow any deduction for business entertainment.

10 Ontario should improve compliance by:

    a) simplifying rules and administrative procedures to make compliance with tax laws easier for taxpayers;

    b) increasing rates of audit and penalties to increase the risk associated with non-compliance;

    c) making the public aware of the enforcement of tax compliance;

    d) improving cooperation among tax authorities within the provincial government and among levels of government to enforce tax compliance;

Recommendations

e) emphasizing cooperative efforts with other levels of government in identifying underground economic activities; and

f) devising special enforcement, reporting, and withholding requirements to address compliance problems in particular areas of the underground economy.

Strengthening Ontario's Role in Income Tax Policy

11 Ontario should seek amendments to the federal-provincial Tax Collection Agreements that permit it to:

a) levy its tax directly on the income base rather than the "tax-on-tax" arrangement currently in place;

b) determine the number of income tax brackets and the rates applicable to them independently of the federal government; and

c) define and determine the value of its own tax credits independently of the federal government.

12 Ontario should seek amendments to the federal-provincial Tax Collection Agreements that allow both levels of government to determine tax expenditures independently by:

a) ensuring they are in the form of tax credits rather than deductions, exemptions, or exclusions from the base; and/or

b) empowering the provincial government to define an "adjusted income" base that would enable it to add items back into its base that the federal government chooses to exclude.

13 Ontario should seek amendments to the federal-provincial Tax Collection Agreements that give it a role in income tax policy and administration by:

a) providing for direct input by the provincial government into the audit and enforcement activities of the federal government involving Ontario taxpayers; and

b) institutionalizing formal consultation in advance of any federal decision affecting the definition of the income tax base.

Equality of Women and Men

14 To continue the recognition in the tax system of the economic independence of men and women, the individual should be retained as the unit of taxation in both the federal and provincial income tax systems.

15 If Ontario gains more control over its personal income tax system through amendments to the federal-provincial Tax Collection Agreements, Ontario should eliminate the marital credit and redirect the funds through a reformed credit system.

16 Ontario should seek the agreement of the federal government to abolish the deduction for child support and alimony payments in the personal income tax. These payments should not be taxable in the hands of the recipient.

The Role of the Tax System in Social Policy

17 Ontario should consolidate the adult components of the Ontario property and sales tax credits and the Ontario Tax Reduction program into a new and simplified Ontario Tax Assistance Credit. The credit should be refundable, delivering its maximum benefit to adults below a specified family income level and declining as income rises.

18 The current system of tax-delivered assistance to families with children through the Ontario Tax Reduction and the sales tax credit should be rationalized into an Ontario child tax credit. The credit would be refundable and provide a declining benefit as family income rises.

19 If Ontario gains more control over its personal income tax system through amendments to the federal-provincial Tax Collection Agreements, the equivalent-to-married credit should be eliminated and replaced with a supplement to the child tax credit that would provide benefits to single parent families.

20 If Ontario establishes an income-tested child benefit program which provides benefits to low-income families regardless of the source of their income, Ontario should not implement the child tax credit proposed in recommendation 18. The assistance to families with children currently delivered through the tax system, through the Ontario Tax Reduction and the sales tax credit, should be eliminated and the additional revenue used to augment the benefits delivered under the child benefit program.

21 If Ontario gains more control over its personal income tax system through amendments to the federal-provincial Tax Collection Agreements, Ontario should eliminate the child care expense deduction and use the revenue recovered in direct program spending for child care.

22 If Ontario gains more control over its personal income tax system through amendments to the federal-provincial Tax Collection Agreements, Ontario should eliminate the disability tax credit and replace it with a flat rate, taxable benefit payable to all persons with disabilities.

23 If Ontario gains more control over its personal income tax system through amendments to the federal-provincial Tax Collection Agreements, Ontario should eliminate the credit for disability-related medical expenses and the deduction for attendant care. In their place, Ontario should establish a program outside the tax system to subsidize the cost of attendant care or medical expenses for persons with a disability.

24 If Ontario gains more control over its personal income tax system through amendments to the federal-provincial Tax Collection Agreements, Ontario should eliminate the age tax credit and replace it with a seniors tax credit. This credit should be refundable and provide a declining benefit as family income rises.

25 If Ontario gains more control over its personal income tax system through amendments to the federal-provincial Tax Collection Agreements, Ontario should eliminate the pension income credit. The revenue recovered by eliminating this credit should be used to increase the value of the seniors tax credit.

26 The maximum retirement benefit eligible for tax assistance through the deduction for contributions to registered pension plans and Registered Retirement Savings Plans in the personal income tax and the deduction of contributions in the corporate income tax is currently 2.5 times the average industrial wage. Ontario should seek the agreement of the federal government to reduce this limit to 1.5. This lower limit should be phased in by freezing the pension maximum and corresponding contribution limits at current levels until the maximum pension and corresponding limits are equivalent to 1.5 times the average industrial wage. Thereafter, contribution limits should be indexed to maintain the ratio.

27 Ontario should seek the agreement of the federal government to convert the deductions for contributions to registered pension plans and RRSPs in the personal income tax and corporate income tax to tax credits. Withdrawals from plans should continue to be taxed as ordinary income.

Taxation of Dividends and Capital Gains

28 Ontario should discuss with the federal government the effectiveness and fairness of the dividend tax credit with a view to eliminating or restructuring the credit, subject to appropriate measures to ensure that small business income is subject to the same amount of tax whether it is earned directly through self-employment or a partnership, or indirectly through a Canadian-controlled private corporation.

29 Ontario should seek the agreement of the federal government to end the exclusion of 25 per cent of capital gains from taxable income. Similarly, all capital gains should be included in corporate income for corporate income tax purposes.

30 Ontario should seek the agreement of the federal government to abolish both the $100,000 general lifetime exemption for capital gains and the special $500,000 lifetime exemptions for farming and small business assets. If the federal government does not agree to make the changes at the federal level, Ontario should make the changes in the Ontario income tax.

The Income Tax Rate

31 If Ontario gains more control over its personal income tax system through amendments to the federal-provincial Tax Collection Agreements, Ontario should adopt a personal income tax rate schedule with the following features:

Recommendations

- a basic personal credit determined by multiplying the lowest Ontario personal income tax rate by the basic personal amount in the federal personal income tax;
- a rate schedule that is graduated over the middle-income range;
- a top marginal rate which would result in a combined federal/provincial top marginal rate of no more than 60 per cent and which would apply to annual taxable income in excess of $250,000; and
- no more than 10 tax brackets.

Taxation of Wealth

32 Ontario should seek the agreement of the federal government and the other provinces to establish a national wealth transfer tax. This tax should be fully comprehensive and should apply to gifts as well as transfers at death. The tax should exempt spousal transfers. It should have a generous exemption level but should contain no credit for capital gains taxes on deemed dispositions.

33 If a wealth transfer tax is implemented which generates additional revenue for the Government of Ontario, Ontario's probate fee should be levied as a user fee at a flat rate, rather than as a percentage of the estate.

Corporate Taxation in a Fair Tax System

34 Ontario should maintain effective rates of tax on business at approximately their current levels relative to other jurisdictions, given the evidence with respect to:
- effective tax rates in competing jurisdictions,
- the impact of effective tax rates on business location decisions, and
- the shifting of corporate taxes to employees, consumers, and investors.

35 It would be desirable in principle to change the composition of taxes on business by increasing taxes based on profitability and decreasing taxes that are not sensitive to profit. However, the fact that the corporate income tax base can move from country to country in response to statutory tax rate differentials means that it is unlikely that increased revenue could be raised through higher corporate income tax rates. The Ontario government should consider the potential for tax base mobility when setting corporate income tax rates.

36 Ontario should seek agreements with the federal and provincial governments to minimize interprovincial tax competition. Agreements should provide for such measures as:
- consolidated taxation in which the tax-paying unit would include all the Canadian members of a corporate group; and
- minimum provincial corporate tax rates.

37 National and subnational jurisdictions face constraints in their ability to tax the income of multinational corporations. While respecting those constraints in establishing its own policy, Ontario should urge the federal government to play an active role in promoting initiatives, such as international tax agreements, to ensure that the income of multinational corporations is taxed fairly.

38 Ontario should not attempt to use its corporate tax system as a mechanism for delivering incentives that are more generous than those offered in the federal system. Corporate tax deductions in Ontario which are either in addition to federal deductions or accelerated compared with federal deductions should be eliminated.

39 In addition to the criteria applicable to tax expenditures generally, tax expenditures designed to further general economic development goals should meet the same criteria that apply to economic development programs delivered outside the tax system:
a) Subsidies should be focused on desired activities or behaviours, not on sectors, types of companies, or size of businesses.
b) The activities or behaviours targeted must be defined and measured easily.
c) The incentives given should be large enough to result in changed corporate decisions.
d) The subsidy programs must be simple to understand and transparent for both companies and the administrative authorities.

e)   To limit the potential for abuse, tax incentives in the form of non-refundable credits should not be tradable among firms but rather should be restricted to the recipient company.

f)   All subsidy programs should be reviewed in depth with potential recipient firms for their likely impact on behaviour before they are introduced.

40 Ontario should eliminate the bias in the corporate income tax against income generated in service industries by removing the preferential rate for profits from manufacturing and processing.

Taxation of Small Business and Cooperatives

41 Ontario should maintain a tax rate lower than the general corporate tax rate for the first $200,000 of small business income. The small business rate should be adjusted periodically to ensure equal tax treatment of small business income received by individuals that has been earned through either an incorporated or an unincorporated business.

42 Ontario should retain the exemption and graduated set of flat rates for the Ontario capital tax in its current form.

43 Ontario should encourage the federal and provincial governments to consider the ownership and governing structure of cooperatives when developing tax policy, programs, and legislation.
Programs should be structured so that:
a)   the requirements can be met as easily by cooperatives as by other enterprises, and
b)   the benefits are equally available to cooperatives and other enterprises.

44 Ontario should amend the worker ownership component of the Ontario Investment and Worker Ownership Program to permit employees to operate a worker-owned enterprise as a cooperative.

45 Ontario should ensure that property held by not-for-profit housing cooperatives be assessed on the same basis, whether they own or lease the land.
Ontario should amend the Land Transfer Tax Act to ensure that it is not applied to the value of the building of a newly developed housing cooperative when the land and the building originate with different corporations.

Payroll Taxation

46 Ontario should eliminate the graduated rate structure for its existing payroll tax and replace it with a uniform rate of tax based on all remuneration.

47 Ontario should establish a new method of calculating remuneration for payroll tax purposes for owner-managers of corporations and self-employed individuals. For owner-managers of corporations, remuneration above an exemption level up to a threshold amount, whether in the form of salary or dividends, should be fully taxable. Above this threshold amount, a portion of remuneration would be excluded from the base as an allowance for the owner-manager's return on capital. For self-employed individuals, a portion of remuneration above the threshold amount would be excluded from the base as an allowance for the return on capital included in earnings.

48 Ontario should seek the agreement of the federal government to make payroll taxes fully deductible for corporate income tax purposes.

Resource Taxation

49 The Ontario Mining Tax should be changed from its current format as a tax on profits to one on cash flow, which would:
a)   allow for the immediate deduction of all capital and operating expenditures;
b)   provide for any expenditures not deducted in the current period to be carried forward with an investment allowance for deduction in future periods; and
c)   exclude any further deduction for depreciation or interest.

Recommendations

Since these features allow full credit for returns on processing assets, there would be no justification for the processing allowance provided for in the current tax format.

50 The resource allowance in the Ontario corporate income tax should be restricted to the lesser of resource taxes actually paid and 25 per cent of resource profits.

51 In establishing rates of tax on cash flow in the mining industry, Ontario should monitor closely world economic conditions in the province's key mineral sectors to ensure that Ontario generates the maximum revenue possible from the underlying value of the mineral resources consistent with the need to maintain the long-term viability of the industry.

Ontario should set the initial rate of the tax on cash flow to generate a long-term revenue yield – after allowing for any additional incentives for exploration, research, and environmental costs – equivalent to the yield of the current tax on profits.

52 A mining tax based on a cash flow format should not provide for:
   a)   exemptions for cash flow below a threshold or on any basis; or
   b)   tax holidays for new mines or on any other basis.

53 Ontario should explore further the potential role for a tax on cash flow in enhancing Ontario's return from its forestry wealth.

54 Ontario should increase its reliance on auctions of forest-harvesting rights to recover the public value of forest products until such time as a cash flow tax can be introduced.

55 Regeneration costs borne by the forestry operation should be deductible from the cash flow base. Regeneration costs borne by the government should be a charge against cash flow prior to the application of the tax.

56 Ontario should revise the system of area charges for forestry to reflect the cost of holding forest land out of alternative uses such as recreation and to reflect costs of administration and forest maintenance.

Retail Sales Tax

57 Ontario should broaden the base of the retail sales tax to include all goods and services with limited exemptions.

58 Ontario should exempt all business inputs from the retail sales tax.

59 Ontario should replace its current single-stage sales tax, levied only at the final point of sale at the retail level, with a multi-stage sales tax levied on all transactions with full credit for tax paid on business inputs.

60 Given the existence of a comprehensive sales tax at the federal level, Ontario should harmonize its retail sales tax with a national sales tax modelled on the federal Goods and Services Tax. This would involve accepting the basic structure of the GST as a multi-stage sales tax or value-added tax, with the following provisions:
   a)   an exemption for health care services, financial services, education services, child care services, personal care services, legal aid, resale of homes, and residential rents; and
   b)   zero-rating for basic groceries, prescription drugs, medical services, transportation services, and public transit services.

In negotiating its participation in a national sales tax system, Ontario should:
   •   examine approaches to making prepared foods purchased in convenience and grocery stores taxable; and
   •   explore the options for including financial services in the tax base.

61 Ontario should require joint administration of the harmonized sales tax, which would provide for:
   a)   joint establishment of all aspects of sales tax policy, with the exception of rates;
   b)   establishment of tax rates by each government independently;
   c)   formal provincial involvement in the administration of the tax. This involvement would be accomplished through recognition of a clearly specified provincial role in the administration of the joint tax;

Recommendations

provincial administration of the joint tax; or establishment of an independent federal/provincial agency for the administration of the joint tax.

62 Ontario should not increase retail sales tax rates on selected luxury items or introduce a distinct excise tax on luxury items.

The Role of Taxes in Protecting the Environment

63 Ontario should increase its reliance on tax-related economic instruments directed towards pollution control. Ontario should establish pollution taxes on substances selected from generally recognized pollutants or lists of recognized pollutants, such as:

- the Primary List of substances for ban or phase-out maintained by the Ontario Ministry of Environment and Energy;
- the Ministry of Environment and Energy Secondary List; or
- the National Pollutant Release Inventory.

Such pollution taxes should apply to all discharges, whether into water (including sewers), land, or air. Such taxes should increase with the quantity of pollution and vary with the risks associated with the discharge of each substance.

In determining the appropriate mix of tax, regulation, and other instruments, Ontario should consider the extent to which the tax can be applied directly to the activities generating the pollution and the potential impact of each type of measure on industrial activity.

64 Ontario should introduce a tax on all fossil fuels consumed in the residential, commercial and industrial, and transportation sectors based on the carbon content of fossil fuel energy inputs. For the largest sources of carbon dioxide emissions, carbon dioxide emission limits should be negotiated and established through regulated limits. The tax should apply to those sources only if they fail to meet agreed emission limits within the established timetable.

65 To maintain incentives for fuel conservation and to reflect the higher environmental costs associated with transportation use, Ontario should retain a rate of tax on transportation fuels higher than on energy consumed in other sectors.

66 Ontario should extend the Tax for Fuel Conservation to light trucks and vans and then adjust the rates to provide a stronger incentive to purchase fuel-efficient vehicles.

67 Ontario should establish a new system of vehicle registration based on mileage, vehicle inspection results, and other vehicle characteristics related to road use, such as weight. Fees raised from this system should replace a portion of the revenue currently raised from transportation fuel taxes. Until this system is implemented, transportation fuel taxes should remain at their current levels.

68 Ontario should introduce an environmental tax on all ozone-depleting substances used in the province, whether new or recycled. The government should ensure that the tax closely complements the province's existing and emerging regulatory framework.

Environmental Charges for Water and Sewer Services and Solid Waste

69 User fees should be applied for water and sewer services, based on levels of consumption and costs of providing the service. Such fees should apply to all sectors that consume these services.

Fees for water and sewer services should include a fixed amount to account for the costs of capital replacement, and a variable amount that reflects consumption.

To improve efficiency and to provide incentives for resource conservation, the user fee system should incorporate such features as peak-load pricing, seasonal pricing, and surcharges for hard-to-treat industrial, commercial, and institutional waste.

User fee systems should include such options as reduced, flat, or constant unit rates up to a minimum level of consumption, subsidized rates for basic service, and exemptions for low-income consumers to ensure that higher fees for sewer and water services do not bar low-income families from access to those services.

70 Ontario should expand the application of user fees for both residential and non-residential solid waste.

71 User fee rates for solid waste in the residential sector should reflect all costs associated with the collection and disposal of solid waste, including the environmental costs generated by waste collection and disposal. Fees should vary with the amount of waste generated. Where possible, fees for residential solid waste should increase with weight.

To ensure broad access to solid waste collection and disposal services, user fee structures should provide for reduced rates for basic service, and special reduced rates for low-income consumers.

72 Ontario should establish a regulatory and fee framework to ensure that prices charged for solid waste collection and disposal in the industrial, commercial, and institutional sector provide incentives for waste reduction.

73 Ontario should introduce a broad-based system of environmental excise taxes on food and beverage containers. These taxes should be fully refundable for containers returned for reuse and partially refunded for containers returned for recycling.

Paying for Services: Property Taxes in a Fair Tax System

74 The provincial government should assume responsibility for the funding of education to a provincial standard, allocating funds to school boards based on per student cost, student needs, and community characteristics which affect education costs, such as poverty and language.

75 Ontario should replace the local residential property tax as a source of core funding for education with funds raised from provincial general revenues.

76 Ontario should eliminate the local education levy on commercial and industrial property.

77 Ontario should permit school boards to raise funds to support local discretionary spending through a local levy on the residential property tax base. The amount of this local levy for each board should be restricted to a fixed percentage – not greater than 10 per cent – of the total amount of provincial funding provided to that board.

78 Ontario should assume full responsibility for funding general welfare assistance and provincially mandated services to children.

79 a) To ensure that municipal governments do not eliminate property tax savings resulting from reform in the funding of education and social services by raising municipal tax rates, those tax rates should be subject to provincial regulation during a transitional period.

b) Ontario should establish a base year municipal tax rate, which excludes taxes attributable to services no longer funded from property taxes, and should limit municipal tax rate increases to a provincial standard increase, subject to appeal. In addition, municipal governments should be required to disclose on their tax bills any increases in tax relative to this revised base year tax rate.

80 Ontario should require that municipalities levy user fees for sewer and water services. Assessment-based charges for water and sewer services should be replaced by metering of all consumption. Flat rate water charges should not be permitted.

81 By the funding of pilot projects and other means, Ontario should encourage municipalities to levy user fees for waste collection.

A New Basis for Property Taxation

82 Residential assessment of individual properties for local taxation purposes should be based on the following factors:
- size of building,
- dimensions of lot, and
- type of building.

Weighting factors used in combining the factors of size of building and dimensions of lot for each type of building should be designed to ensure that the resulting assessments reflect variations in the value of properties in their current use, as shown in their rental value.

Weighting factors would be permitted to vary, based on location, subject to the following requirements:

- Without differential weighting factors based on location, it would be impossible to achieve assessments which reflect value in current use.
- Assessment areas could not be smaller than geographically contiguous areas which carry the same zoning designation for planning purposes.

83 Residential tenants should be made aware of the assessment and corresponding property taxes that apply to the property they occupy and that are reflected in their rents. Municipalities should be required to send property tax notices to all tenants, informing them of all taxes applicable to their units.

Administrative mechanisms should be developed to ensure that landlords are able to pass on increases in property tax and that tenants receive full credit in their rents for any reductions in property tax that result from reform of local government financing.

Local government finance reforms affecting residential rental property should not be implemented until such a mechanism has been developed.

84 All recreational vehicles and trailers located permanently in a campground or trailer park should be assessed as residential property. Location would be considered permanent if the mobility of the vehicle or trailer is impaired. Vehicles and trailers located in a campground or trailer park for more than 30 days and not assessed should be subject to a monthly fee. The fee should be established by the provincial government to approximate the local taxes that would apply if the structure were a permanent dwelling, pro-rated to a monthly amount.

Fees would be collected by the operator and remitted to the local municipality or local roads board.

85 Non-residential property should be assessed on the basis of the rental value of the property – the price that would be paid for property of that class and type for the right to employ the property in its current use.

86 Statutory assessment rates should apply to non-residential properties whose value in current use is difficult to determine.

Railway, pipeline, and electrical transmission rights of way should be assessed at provincial standard unit rates which are updated on a regular basis as assessed values generally are updated.

Church sanctuaries and cemeteries should be assessed at a standard unit rate.

87 Vacant land should be assessed based on the preponderant use of property in the area. Vacant land includes surface parking lots zoned for other purposes and unused rights of way.

Municipal Taxation Policy

88 All residential property should be assessed on the same basis whether the property is occupied by an owner or a tenant.

89 Non-commercial cottage and recreational property should be assessed as residential property and be subject to local municipal taxes on exactly the same basis as other residential property.

90 Local levies for education should apply to all properties assessed and taxed for municipal purposes as residential property, including non-commercial cottage and recreational property.

91 Ontario should allow municipal governments to establish their own rates of tax on non-residential property, subject to a minimum rate of tax established by the provincial government.

92 The farm residence and one acre of land should be assessed and fully taxed as residential property.

93 Wetlands, managed forests, and farming property other than the farm residence and one acre should be assessed as non-residential property based on its value in current use, established using available provincial data on soil quality and productivity, and should be subject to local non-residential property taxes.

94 The business occupancy tax should be abolished as a separate form of taxation of non-residential property.

Municipal governments should have explicit powers to replace the revenue forgone from residential or non-residential property taxes.

95 To replace the relief provided for vacant non-residential properties in the current non-residential and business occupancy tax systems, the local non-residential tax rate should be reduced by 40 per cent for property that is vacant.

96 Ontario should develop general legislation regarding exemptions from local property taxes and should repeal the exemption provisions of existing private legislation.

Property should be exempt from local taxation only if it is determined that the owner should not be required to pay for local services or if there is a public policy rationale for linking a subsidy directly to the amount of property tax paid on the property.

Exemptions should be based on the nature of the use of a property rather than on the characteristics of the owner of the property.

Municipal governments should not have the power to exempt property from taxation.

97 Crown land should continue to be exempt from local property taxation, but should be subject to full payment by the province in lieu of all local property taxes, based on the assessment of similar property. Roads and highways should not be subject to taxation or to payments in lieu of taxes.

98 The exemption from local property taxation for "property held in trust for a band or body of Indians" should be restricted to reserve lands and other lands for which municipal services are not provided.

99 Public hospitals and public educational institutions should continue to be exempt from local property taxation. Formula payments in lieu of taxes based on the number of beds or the number of students should be eliminated and replaced by full payment in lieu of taxes by the province based on the assessment of similar property.

100 The exemption from local property taxation for Children's Aid Societies should be continued. The provincial government should make payments in lieu of taxes for Children's Aid Societies.

101 The property of lower-tier (local) municipalities and school boards located within their geographic jurisdiction should be exempt from local property taxes. Property of upper-tier municipalities (regional, district, and metropolitan municipalities and counties), other than roads, highways, and public transit rights of way, should be subject to local property taxes.

102 The local property tax exemptions for public libraries and agricultural and horticultural societies should be restricted to property owned and operated by a municipal government or an agency of a municipal government and located within the municipality.

103 The local property tax exemptions should be eliminated for property owned, occupied, and used by: the Boy Scouts Association; the Canadian Girl Guides Association; private reform schools and orphanages; charitable organizations for the relief of the poor; the Canadian Red Cross Society; and the St. John Ambulance Association.

104 The local property tax exemptions for churches, cemeteries, and religious and educational seminaries should be eliminated.

105 The local property tax exemption for battle sites should be eliminated.

106 Other local property tax exemptions should be limited to property owned and used by institutions of provincial interest or importance. The provincial government should make full payments in lieu of taxes for all such exempt property.

107 The following transitional rules should apply to the repeal of existing exemptions from property taxation:
   a) After advance notice of one year, there should be a phase-in period of up to five years to permit taxpayers to adjust.
   b) Exemption policies should only be changed following the introduction of assessment based on value in current use for commercial and industrial properties and unit value assessment for residential properties.

Recommendations

c) Special statutory assessment rates should be established for exempt properties for which it is impossible to determine a value in current use, such as the portion of church property used as a sanctuary.

d) Properties such as cemeteries which are supported by fixed endowments based on tax exempt status should continue to be exempt. New cemeteries established after the change in policy should be taxable.

108 The special local property tax exemption for mining buildings and machinery located underground should be eliminated. Any building, machinery, or equipment that would be taxable if located on the surface should be taxable if located underground.

109 The exemption from local property taxation for up to 20 acres of forestry land attached to a farm (a wood lot) should be eliminated. Such property should be assessed and taxed based on its value in use as a wood lot.

110 Provided a unit value residential assessment system is adopted, in which assessments of individual properties of the same type and in the same geographic area vary only with differences in physical dimensions, exemption from local property taxation for modifications to property for the accommodation of elderly or disabled residents should be eliminated; any appropriate assistance should be provided through direct spending programs.

Making the Local Financial System Work Better

111 Ontario should limit provincial grants and subsidies to municipal governments in areas of local jurisdiction to:

a) areas in which the province wishes to increase local spending because such spending generates spillover benefits outside the local area or in the province generally; and

b) areas in which it is considered appropriate that the province guarantee the availability of a basic level of service, regardless of local fiscal capacity.

Grants intended to increase levels of local spending on programs that generate benefits for people who live outside the local area (spillover benefits) should be designed to provide assistance for spending above minimum levels rather than matching funding from the first dollar spent.

112 Ontario's subsidy programs for municipal governments should be targeted to deal with factors that limit the ability of municipalities to provide access to adequate local services at reasonable cost. These programs should focus on particular local services; should be based on factors such as climate, geography, and density of population; and should be designed to respond to emergency situations, such as the closure of a business vital to the local revenue base.

To ensure that assistance is available only to offset excessive local tax burdens required to fund minimum standard services, subsidies under such programs should vary based on local fiscal capacity – the ability of the municipality to raise revenue to pay for those programs while imposing a reasonable burden on local taxpayers.

Local fiscal capacity should be measured separately for the residential and non-residential sectors. For the non-residential sector, local fiscal capacity should be measured using assessment, adjusted by equalization factors so that it is measured on the same basis throughout Ontario. For the residential sector, local fiscal capacity should be measured based on residential property taxes paid by residents of the municipality as a proportion of the total income of all households in the municipality.

Subsidies should equalize the impact on household incomes in the municipality of residential property taxes required to support a particular service, after allowing for local revenue from the application of a standard effective rate of tax on commercial and industrial properties and after allowing for revenue from the taxation of residential property used by non-residents.

113 Each local (lower-tier) municipality's share of county, regional, district, or metropolitan (upper-tier) costs should be based on its share of total residential and non-residential assessment.

Residential and non-residential assessment would be measured on a consistent basis throughout the upper-tier area. The share of each lower-tier municipality would be determined as follows:

a) The weighted average rate of tax on residential property in the upper-tier area in the previous year would be calculated by dividing total residential property taxes levied for upper-tier purposes by all municipalities in the upper-tier area by total residential assessment in the upper-tier area.

b) The weighted average rate of tax on non-residential property in the upper-tier area in the previous year would be calculated by dividing total non-residential property taxes levied for upper-tier purposes by all municipalities in the upper-tier area by total non-residential assessment in the upper-tier area.

c) Residential assessment would be multiplied by the weighted average rate of tax on residential property as calculated above.

d) Non-residential assessment would be multiplied by the weighted average rate of tax on non-residential property as calculated above.

e) The share of each municipality would be calculated by adding the figures obtained in (c) and (d) above and dividing by total residential and non-residential property taxes for upper-tier purposes in the upper-tier area in the previous year.

Once the share of each lower-tier municipality is determined in this fashion, lower-tier municipalities would determine the mix of residential and non-residential property taxes used to raise the required revenue in accordance with their own taxation policies.

114 Development charges for education should be eliminated, and the infrastructure costs associated with education should be funded from provincial general revenues.

Municipal development charges should not apply to infrastructure development that is related solely to the total population of the municipality, irrespective of its location within the municipality, and should apply only to costs that would not be recovered from increased property taxes on the new development.

Provincial Property Taxation

115 Ontario should establish a provincial property tax on commercial and industrial property, levied at a uniform effective rate across the province, to replace the revenue raised by the local education levy on non-residential property and the education share of the business occupancy tax.

116 The provincial commercial and industrial tax should be levied on the assessed value of commercial and industrial property as established for municipal taxation purposes and equalized to a common base across Ontario.

117 The provincial commercial and industrial property tax should apply to all non-residential property which is used for a business purpose. Property owned by a non-profit organization and used for a non-profit or charitable purpose should be exempt from the provincial commercial and industrial property tax.

118 Provincial policy towards the taxation of farming should be reformed as follows:

a) Farming property should be exempt from the provincial commercial and industrial property tax pending a broader review of the economics of the farming industry in Ontario and the policy objectives of government with respect to the farming industry.

b) The Farm Tax Rebate Program should be abolished.

119 The rate for the provincial commercial and industrial tax should be set to generate approximately the same amount of revenue as is currently raised for education at the local level from the business occupancy tax and the non-residential property tax.

Reducing Reliance on Regressive Taxes

120 Ontario should reduce its reliance on residential property taxes.

121 Ontario should increase its reliance on revenue from personal income taxes.

Recommendations

122 Ontario should meet the additional requirements for funding resulting from reform of education finance and the assumption by the provincial government of responsibility for funding of services for children as follows:

Residential ($ billions)

Education property taxes		4.600	
LESS	Local levy	0.727	
	Grants offset (net)	0.373	
Property tax reduction			**3.500**
To be replaced by			
PIT rate changes		3.000	
Sales tax base		0.300	
Payroll tax changes		0.150	
Corporate income tax			
uniform rate		0.050	
Additional revenue			**3.500**

Commercial and industrial ($ billions)

Education property taxes		3.095	
LESS	Grants offset (net)	0.251	
Local property tax change			**2.844**
To be replaced by			
Provincial commercial and			
industrial tax			**2.844**

123 If Ontario gains more control over its personal income tax system through amendments to the federal-provincial Tax Collection Agreements, it should raise the revenue necessary to meet the tax mix objectives recommended by the Fair Tax Commission by establishing the following rate schedule and credit amounts:
* brackets and marginal rates

Taxable Income ($)	Rate (%)
10,000 and under	10
10,001–20,000	12
20,001–29,590	14
29,591–40,000	16
40,001–50,000	18
50,001–59,180	20
59,181–80,000	22
80,001–150,000	24
150,001–250,000	26
Over 250,000	28

* a basic personal credit with the amount claimed equal to the federal amount and the credit rate equal to the lowest Ontario marginal tax rate.

124 Refundable credit amounts should be as follows:
* an Ontario tax assistance credit of $500 per adult family member up to family income of $18,000, and reduced at a rate of 8.3 per cent of income in excess of $18,000;
* an additional Ontario tax assistance credit of $300 for individuals aged 65 and over;
* a child tax credit of $600 for the first child and $500 for each additional child, up to a family income of $18,000 and reduced at a rate of 7.5 per cent of income in excess of $18,000;
* an additional credit of $400 for the first child in a single parent family.

If Ontario establishes an income-tested child benefit which provides benefits to families with children regardless of the family's source of income, the child tax benefit should be eliminated and folded into this new program.

Tax Considerations in Aboriginal Self-government

125 Ontario should declare its readiness to negotiate tax harmonization accords with aboriginal governments and to help develop administrative arrangements to facilitate taxation by aboriginal governments.

Implementation and Transition

126 Ontario should proceed with proposed changes in the structure of its income tax credit system at its earliest opportunity.

127 Ontario should develop a coordinated strategy for negotiating with the federal government on:
a) changes in the personal income tax collection agreement;
b) reform in the tax treatment of child support and alimony;
c) reform in the tax treatment of income from capital;
d) sales tax harmonization;
e) wealth transfer taxation; and
f) a framework agreement on the income tax treatment of federal, provincial, and local taxes paid by corporations.

These changes should be part of general negotiations on federal-provincial fiscal arrangements.

128 Ontario should implement the recommended changes in education expenditure allocation and in the sources of revenue for education as a package.

An education finance reform package must also include a mechanism to ensure that property tax reductions on residential rental property are passed on to tenants and must enable municipalities to set tax rates on residential and non-residential property independently.

129 Ontario must introduce a complete framework for education finance at the beginning of the transition to a new funding system.

This framework should include the expenditure allocation model, the shift in commercial and industrial taxation responsibility from school boards to the province, legislative authority for the discretionary local levy on residential property, and the shift in primary funding responsibility for education from school boards to the provincial government.

130 The education portion of the residential property tax (other than the limited local discretionary levy) should be eliminated at the beginning of the phase-in period.

The shift from local non-residential property taxes for education to provincial commercial and industrial taxation at a uniform rate should be phased in over a five-year period.

131 Prior to the beginning of the transition period for assessment reform, Ontario should implement policy changes dealing with local tax policy flexibility; with sharing the costs of regional, district, and metropolitan municipalities and counties among local municipalities; and with the establishment of a new basis for distributing provincial equalization grants among municipalities.

132 Transitional and implementation measures for local government finance reform should be consistent with the following criteria:
a) Transition should take place over a defined period of time; it should not be linked to an event such as the sale of property (in the case of assessment) or subsequent decision by a particular local government.
b) Transition should, to the extent possible, be weighted towards the beginning of the transitional period to ensure that momentum for reform is maintained.

The same transitional measures should apply to all classes of property.

133 Ontario should, if possible, implement the reform of education finance and of commercial and industrial assessment at the same time.

134 In the transition period for assessment reform, the old and reformed assessment rolls should be maintained in parallel. Over a fixed transition period, municipalities would raise a portion of their revenue requirements from the old assessment roll and a portion from the new assessment roll, with the proportions mandated to shift towards the new roll throughout the transition period.

Business occupancy taxes would be phased out by linking them to the old assessment roll only.

135 Ontario should locate all of the functions related to local government finance in one ministry.

Recommendations

APPENDIX B
REFERENCES

The material in the document is taken from the report of the Fair Tax Commission. Sources for all facts and figures appearing in the Highlights are found in the report. Sources of direct quotations used in the Highlights follow:

Arthur, John, and William H. Shaw, eds. 1978. *Justice and Economic Distribution*. Englewood Cliffs, N.J.: Prentice-Hall

Canada. Department of Finance. 1991. *The Budget, 1991; Budget Papers Tabled in the House of Commons ... February 26, 1991*. Ottawa

Dahlby, Bev. 1993. "Payroll Taxes." In *Business Taxation in Ontario*, ed. Allan M. Maslove, 80–170. Fair Tax Commission, Research Studies. Toronto: University of Toronto Press

Daly, Michael. 1992. "Harmonization of Corporate Taxes in a Single European Market: Recent Developments and Prospects." *Canadian Tax Journal*, 40(5): 1051–85

Hare, R.M. 1978. "Justice and Equality." In *Justice and Economic Distribution*, ed. J. Arthur and W. H. Shaw, 116–31. Englewood Cliffs, N.J.: Prentice Hall

Kesselman, Jonathan R. n.d. "Compliance, Enforcement, and Administrative Factors in Improving Tax Fairness." In *Issues in the Taxation of Individuals*, ed. Allan M. Maslove. Fair Tax Commission, Research Studies. Toronto: University of Toronto Press. Forthcoming

Reich, Robert B. 1988. "Policy Making in a Democracy." In *The Power of Public Ideas*, ed. R. Reich, 123–56. Cambridge: Ballinger Publishing